Copyright © 2018 by Joshua

The author has used his best this material. The author and publisher make no representations or warranties as to the applicability, fitness, accuracy, or completeness of this and accompanying materials. They disclaim any warranties (express or implied), merchantability or applicability for any particular purpose. The author and publisher shall in no event be held liable for any loss or other damages, including but not limited to special, incidental, consequential, or other damages. As always, the advice of competent legal, tax, accounting or other professional should be sought. The author and publisher do not warrant the performance, effectiveness, or applicability of any sites listed in this book. All links are for information purposes only and are not warranted for content, accuracy or any other implied or explicit purpose. This book contains material protected under International and Federal Copyright Laws and Treaties. Any unauthorized reprint or use of the material is prohibited. All rights reserved. No part of this publication may be reproduced, distributed, or transmitted in any form or by any means, including photocopying, recording, or other electronic or mechanical methods, without the prior written permission of the publisher, except in the case of brief quotations embodied in critical reviews and certain other noncommercial uses permitted by copyright law. For permission requests, write to the publisher, addressed "Attention: Permissions Coordinator," at the address below.

Best Tax Pro, LLC

6040 Main Street, Suite #102

Rockford, MN 55373

Ordering Information

Quantity sales: Special discounts are available on quantity purchases by corporations, associations, and others. For details, contact the publisher at the address above.

Orders by U.S. trade bookstores and wholesalers: Please contact Best Tax Pro, LLC. Tel: (763) 477-4205; Fax: (763) 477-5893

Produced and Printed in the United States of America

Table of Contents

Table Of Contents	iv
Preface	vii
Acknowledgements	xii

PART 1: How to Survive an IRS Audit

Part 1: Section 1 - Audit Selection Screenings

The Letter Arrives	3
Your Tax Return Is Being Audited	5
IRS Makes First Contact	11
Recent Scams	15
Audit Selection Methods	17
The Document Matching Program	18
Someone Else Is Being Audited	19
Computer DIF & UI DIF Scores	19
Random Selection	19

Part 1: Section 2 - Different Types of Audits

HOW Am I Being Audited?	21
What are the different types of IRS audits?	21
Correspondence Audit	23
Office Audit	25
Field Audit	29
National Research Project (NRP) Audit	31

Part 1: Section 3 - Prepare For Your Audit

Organize Your Documents	35
Sample Letter to Reschedule	39
Types Of Documents Requested	41

Schedule C	43
The Three P's	43
Business Expenses - Schedule C	46
Meals & Entertainment	48
Utilities	50
Legal And Professional	51
Supplies	51
Cost Of Goods Sold	52
Insurance	54
Repairs & Maintenance	56
Interest-Other	57
Rent or Lease	58
Office Expenses	58
Business Use Of Home	59
Organization is Key!	63

Part 1: Section 4 - Face-To-Face With the IRS

The Face-To-Face Audit	62
Specific Interview Techniques	66
A Stressful Situation	72
Carefully Thought Out	75

Part 2: How to Survive After an IRS Audit

Part 2: Section 1 - After the Audit

The Audit Report	81
Collection Due Process (CDP)	85
Deadlines - You Snooze, You Lose	91
How Did I Get Here?	93
Appeals	97

Part 2: Section 2 - Collections Alternatives

Consider the Available Options	101

Alternatives to IRS Collections	*105*
Offer in Compromise	*107*
Currently Not Collectible	*111*
Challenge the Underlying Liability	*113*
Payment Programs	*115*
Streamlined Installment Agreements - SIA	*115*
Other Installment Agreements	*117*
Partial-Pay Installment Agreements	*119*
Innocent Spouse Considerations	*121*
Innocent Spouse – IRC § 6015(b)	*122*
Separation of Liability IRC § 6015(c)	*123*
Equitable Relief IRC § 6015(f)	*124*
Penalty Abatement	*127*
The United States Tax Court	*131*
Appendix A - What Are Your Rights?	*139*
Appendix B - Audit Letters	*147*
Appendix C – Collections Letters	*151*
Appendix D – Letters/Notices with Appeals Rights	*158*
Glossary	*164*
Index	*177*

Preface

The real purpose of writing this book has more to do with three of my core values than it does with the topic of IRS procedures for income tax audits, appeals, or alternatives to collections. I learned about the five core values that drive my decision making by reading a book written by Doug Lennick and Fred Kiel, Ph.D. In their book, *Moral Intelligence: Enhancing Business Performance and Leadership Success*, they assert that for each of us, our core values help us to be selective about how we spend our precious time. My five core values are faith, family, health, honesty, and peace of mind. I frequently reflect on these values when I am making an important decision.

Three of my core values: my faith in a higher purpose, my appreciation for honesty and my delight in serving up a sizeable portion of peace of mind to those in distress: the Troubled Taxpayer in the midst of an IRS audit. These three core values have driven me to write this book.

I present:

- The different ways the IRS contacts Truly Troubled Taxpayers,
- How individual tax returns are selected for an IRS audit,

- The different types and variations of IRS tax audits,
- How to best prepare documents in an audit scenario,
- Specific techniques the IRS uses in their audit process,
- What to do if assistance is needed during an audit,
- What's involved after the audit and some potential next steps,
- Some very specific alternatives to collections available after an IRS audit, and
- Several often overlooked steps in properly preparing to go to US Tax Court.

I began writing this book as if it were about getting from the first phase of an audit (right *here*) to a point at the end of an audit and beyond (*there*). In the process, it became apparent to me that I should mention that *every Truly Troubled Taxpayer's tax situation is entirely different*. Add to that the fact that getting from *here* to *there* never seems to follow a straight line. In fact, I find that beginning the discussion of surviving an IRS audit makes more sense by changing my perspective and taking a step back - a BIG step back. (Pause now and take in a deep breath. It may get somewhat spacey.)

From outer space, astronauts are unable to distinguish any of the topographical details of the earth; it looks like a simple sphere. It does not take a tremendous amount of energy to imagine a sphere. Now try to imagine four spheres, each of them having one of the following labels: *IRS Audit, IRS Collections, IRS Appeals, US Tax Court.*

The *IRS Audit Sphere* is a where the IRS reviews financial information reported or omitted on a tax return to ensure that the correct amount of tax is being paid.

The *IRS Collections Sphere* is a where the IRS takes a series of collections actions (sending out letters, notices, property visits, etc.) if you do not voluntarily pay them the taxes they have determined you owe.

The IRS Appeals Sphere is where tax burdens canon the one hand be relieved or on the other get sent back to the *IRS Audit Sphere.*

The *US Tax Court Sphere* has a limited number of doors marked "enter here," and is intended as a final solution, one way or another.

Just as there are multiple steps involved in moving from one planet (Earth) to another (the moon or Mars, for instance), moving from one of these four imaginary spheres to another requires taking several steps in a very specific sequence.

 This book points out and describes in detail some the many different "doorways" allowing movement within the IRS Solar System (i.e. from IRS Audit to IRS Appeals, from IRS Audit to US Tax Court, and/or from IRS Appeals to US Tax Court

Alternatives to IRS Collections are discussed; IRS Collections is not addressed, as this is not an ideal vacation location.

This book references the Internal Revenue Code and Internal Revenue Manual with the intention of helping a Truly Troubled Taxpayer digest the information, answer difficult questions and make informed decisions.

As mentioned on the back cover, I am an Enrolled Agent with over 14 years' experience in dealing with the IRS. The contents of this book reflect the years of experience I have accumulated in representing clients before the IRS in income tax audits, collections, and appeals hearings. I have studied extensively to take and pass the exam for non-attorneys to represent taxpayers before the US Tax Court in November 2018.

For your convenience, the **initial** use of some technical terms appears in <u>bold underlined text</u>. I have alphabetically arranged these highlighted words in a glossary, which appears at the end of this book.

In addition, at certain points in this book there are some small figures in the margin. Here is an explanation of their meaning.

Lightbulb with an exclamation point in the middle – indicates particularly eye-opening passages, tips or hints about an audit topic.

Triangle with an exclamation point in the middle – an alert to be mindful of the technical reminders, direct, and/or indirect message conveyed by the text.

Clipboard with a wrench & hammer in the middle – This symbol is to indicate passages within the text that requires your attnetion and some heavy mental lifting.

Smiley face – Whatever …things probably won't work out the way you think.

 **Teaching Points** – topics addressed in the beginning of each chapter that are covered in more precise detail later on..

I hope you find usefulness and value in the contents of this book.

Acknowledgements

Praise and thanks be to God.

I thank my parents, who taught me the value of hard work and pursuing an education.

This book would not have been possible without the support and encouragement of my lovely wife Janna Webskowski and our two beautiful children, Lukas and Ayva.

A sincere thank you to my editors, Lynn Jacobs, EA, USTCP, JP Gillach, and Robert Johnstone who have all freely and generously given up their valuable time to help me in editing my book at various stages.

Words cannot express my gratitude to illustrator Joel O'Brien Keene for all his hard work and his extraordinary talent.

Many thanks go to the gentle prompting and magnificent support I have received from the members of my study group: Edward Contract, EA; Lynn Jacobs, EA, **USTCP**; Lisa McDonald, EA; and Cindy Peterson, EA. I never would have thought of writing this book without you all.

AUDIT SCREENING SELECTION

The Letter Arrives

As you walk toward the mailbox to get the mail, all is right with the world. You reach out your hand to open the mailbox and suddenly feel a jolt! Your feet leave the ground to the sky as your realize your body is being tipped upside down. You abruptly drop to the ground, landing squarely on the top left portion of your forehead. Your heart is pumping through your chest. The veins in your neck are protruding. Sweat begins to pour down your forehead. Rolling on your side, your hand immediately reaches for the point of impact, your head. A quick glance at your hand confirms your worst fears: a profuse amount of blood is emanating from your body. As you gradually begin to become aware of the severity of your injury, pain takes hold. You take in a deep breath and let go, as your body starts to convulse and you begin to sob uncontrollably. Through your tears, you can see the blurry image of an official-looking envelope. The envelope looks like it is coming from the IRS. After you confirm that your name and address are correct, you open the envelope. As you begin to read, it becomes apparent to you that the IRS is auditing your income tax return from a couple of years ago and you are Cliff, Mr. Cliff Hanger, the Truly Troubled Taxpayer.

Your Tax Return is Being Audited

 *What is an IRS audit, in general?*

An <u>IRS Audit</u>? What does that mean? Many taxpayers receiving a letter from the IRS ask themselves some common questions:

    Are they going to take my house?

    Can they repossess my car?

    Are they going to file a lien against me?

    Will they garnish my paycheck next week?

Is my bank account safe?

Should I move my money out of my current bank account or open up a new bank account at another bank?

If I did not keep all my records, can the IRS send me to jail?

Will I have to meet or speak with the IRS?

 An IRS Audit is an accounting procedure that requires an examiner to ensure that the information that was reported on an individual's (or an organization's) tax return is accurate (based on all currently applicable tax laws).

In doing so, the IRS examiner also verifies that the amount of tax calculated on your tax return is true and correct. Reviewing and examining the individual's (or an organization's) bank accounts and financial records is the common way of ensuring that this information is correct. Something that appeared on a tax return in error (or *should* have appeared on your tax return but did not) may have triggered an alarm somewhere. Now the IRS personnel is charged with determining how much that error adds up to in terms of dollars owed to the US Department of the Treasury. As for the question about spending time in prison, only extreme cases of tax evasion buy you a ticket to the big house (jail).

"But wait!" you say. *"I bought the Speedy Cat Gerbil Tax Software, and they said my return was okay."* The fact that you were brave enough to do your taxes on your own is testament to your ability. However, this book's purpose is to tell you how to survive an IRS audit, not to compare one method of tax preparation over another. Whenever a taxpayer like Cliff Hanger gets a letter from the IRS (a.k.a. the Dark Side), there is always at least one seemingly mysterious reason lurking in the background. At this point, it's anybody's guess, but first things first:

- Cliff Hanger prepared his own tax return or paid for someone else to prepare the tax return, and Cliff's signature authorized that the information on the tax return was true and correct.
- Cliff Hanger submitted his tax return to the IRS computer system.
- The IRS processed the tax return submitted, and this tax return was set aside for audit.
- Mr. Cliff Hanger received a letter from the IRS stating that the IRS is auditing his tax records!

Although it can be hard to swallow, the fact may be that you are the Truly Troubled Taxpayer and that the IRS is investigating you. The IRS (a.k.a. the Agency) is a bureau of the US Department of the Treasury and is regarded by many as a super-secretive federal organization whose methods and agents work behind a shroud of mystery.

 Whether or not that statement is true, as it pertains to their tax return being audited by the IRS, *this precise moment in history* is the time that Cliff, our example of a Truly Troubled Taxpayer, has the biggest opportunity to act, the most options to evaluate as to what to do, and the greatest flexibility to explore where to go next.

When making the decision of what to do next, Cliff Hanger must keep one thing in mind. In addition to just landing on his head at the mailbox, he does not want to expose himself to problems that are too big to imagine.

 To keep from being exposed to a new dimension of pain, always tell the truth to the IRS.

The IRS has all kinds of supporting documents already in their possession to fortify their case against most Truly Troubled Taxpayers. Once Cliff begins to maybe not exactly tell the truth, the IRS acts on the implied meaning behind not telling the truth. The <u>examiner</u> will begin to wonder what else Cliff could be hiding. Even if the IRS does not have anything else to find out because the Cliff has nothing to hide, the IRS examiner will be looking at Cliff with suspicion because his tax return is under audit.

 On multiple occasions, several different examiners have told me during the face-to-face portion of the examination: they work for the Dark Side of the force.

So just be honest and simply tell the truth. Okay? K.

Walking back towards the house with one hand on his forehead and the other holding the letter, Cliff decides that it's probably most important to stop the bleeding first. After being bandaged up at the local clinic, the Cliff's gaze returns to the blood-stained letter, amazingly still in his left hand. Cliff's vision is sort of fuzzed over and just as he begins to read the first line, his cell phone rings. A person on the other side of the line begins to explain, in a thick eastern accent, that he is from the IRS. Evidently, the IRS is going to sue him! If he does not send the money right now, Cliff will go directly to jail. Cliff Hanger, the Truly Troubled Taxpayer, pulls the phone away from his ear to look at it and wonder: *is this how the IRS does things these days?!*

IRS Makes First Contact

 *How are tax returns selected for audit?
What ways can the IRS use to contact taxpayers?*

Phone calls allegedly coming from the IRS have been a recent (circa 2016-2017) method to dishonestly scheme taxpayers out of their hard-earned money. If you get a call from someone purporting to be from the IRS and haven't yet received a letter from them in the mail, tell the person on the phone, who is quite possibly impersonating an IRS employee, to call back after the letter they have sent arrives and then politely say goodbye and hang up the phone.

Although the IRS *may* give you a call before they send you any notice in the mail, contact from the IRS will more than likely come through the mail -- unless you receive a visit from a Revenue Officer (RO) at your home or place of business.

This paying-you-a-visit technique usually happens on a Friday or just before a U.S. Holiday, some of their favorite times to get out of the office in the field.

To ensure that you are aware that an IRS Agent stopped by your house while you were not there, they usually leave a business card in a prominent location: wedged in your door jam, duct-taped to your door, etc. They will also send you a confirmation notice, through the mail, detailing the date and time of their attempt to contact you at your home or place of business.

For the ultimate protection, organize and retain every speck of information received from the IRS.

If you want help in solving your tax problem, your best friend might just be the documents that describe your tax problem to an Enrolled Agent CPA, or Tax Attorney. All IRS Notices or Letters contain a wealth of information. You should study these documents diligently to confirm that the information all appears correct to the best of your knowledge. The IRS sends out some basic types of computer paragraphs, notices, and letters. These are for audits, collections, and general letters regarding return errors and return requests. Some of these same types of letters and notices are sent out to businesses as well.

 For a listing and brief description of some of the more common types of notices and letters issued by the IRS, see *Appendix B*, *Appendix C*, or *Appendix D*.

The notice number in the upper or lower right-hand corner of the letter or notice might begin with the letters "CP" or "LTR" followed by a series of numbers.

 These numbers can provide a clue as to what the specific issue or issues the IRS is examining on a tax return, or they may point to the reason a particular tax return was selected for audit.

Once you know the reason **why** you are being audited, you can narrow your focus. You can begin gathering any and all relevant documents.

It's important to discover if the letter provides you with a "respond by" date. For the IRS, this date is not really important – *unless you disagree with their findings.* If you really do not have a strong desire to pay the amount they have calculated on the letter or you don't believe you owe them at all, the date contained in the letter is **extremely** important.

 The countdown has begun. Time is of the essence.

Good thing I picked up that great book, you think, as you hang up the phone on the IRS impersonator. Being both a conscientious and responsible citizen of the United States of America, you decide that you will send a letter to your elected officials in Washington, D.C. first thing when you get home. There has to be something *they* can do to stop this type of phone scam! It suddenly occurs to you that it'd probably be easier to type your action letter out on your computer. Hey-wait! Everybody's got an email -- including all the senators and representatives! So you decide to stop and get a cup of coffee on the way home and reach out to them with your tablet in comfort. This is going to feel so good! As you open up your browser and navigate to your email provider, you notice a few unread emails. One from your friend at work, one confirming that your utility bill just got auto-paid, and… one of them… is from… the IRS! How can this be? That's impossible!

Recent Scams

 *What different ways does the IRS use to send out notification of an audit?*

Impossible? Correct!

It's not that the agency responsible for tax collection and tax law enforcement doesn't allow any of the IRS examiners to communicate via email, but that's not how the IRS notifies a Troubled Taxpayer that they are being audited

 If you receive a notice from the IRS *via e-mail*, it is more than likely phishing for information or someone trying to scam you.

You can report this to the IRS by calling 1-800-829-1040 and wait on hold for 90 minutes before being given what has become known as a courtesy disconnect. If you prefer to report this to the

IRS electronically, you may also do so via their "Report Phishing and Online Scams" website. If I were you, I would print the offending email for posterity sake, and simply delete it.

After deleting the email *obviously* **NOT** from the IRS, you take a sip of your hot drink you got at the coffee shop and return your gaze to the letter. *How do I know **this** is really from the IRS?* It's on their stationery. It looks official. So you dramatically throw your arms out to your sides, and imagine yelling, **What gives?** , as you spill a little coffee on the arm of the chair. **What did I do wrong to cause such a nasty trip to the Emergency Room—6 stitches in my forehead!—and get audited by the IRS? Why me?** Why. Indeed.

Audit Selection Methods

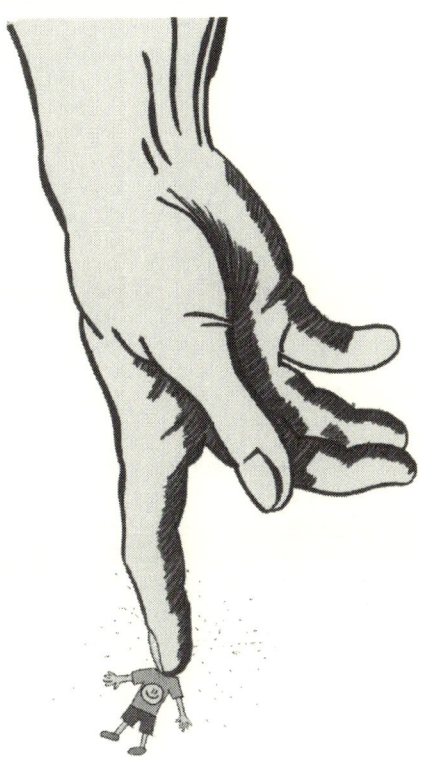

 *How returns are selected for audit*

Why did the IRS pick your return to be audited? Your <u>income tax return</u> can be selected for audit for a variety of different reasons. The 21st century reason for audit selection all boils down to the simple fact that a computer program picked your return, but let's get down to the nitty-gritty.

1. Matching
2. It's somebody else's fault
3. Computer scores
4. The Randomizer

The Document Matching Program - It could be that your wages were paid to you in cash and the person who paid you reported your wages to the IRS as non-employee compensation on a Form 1099. Or you may have received a paycheck each week, every other week, once a month – whatever – and your employer reported the annual wages you were paid to the IRS on a W-2. One of the many computers in an IRS processing center may have found that the wages you reported (or didn't report) on your tax return don't match what was reported to the IRS. The IRS computer system also could have detected some large, unreasonable or questionable deductions (the IRS calls the LUQs for shorthand). These LUQs either don't make sense as they relate to income that was reported to the IRS, or it could be that these LUQs are inconsistent with the amounts of income you reported elsewhere on your return. The list could keep going on and on, but the above examples give you a good idea for why the IRS selects some returns for closer examination in an audit.

Someone else is being audited – The IRS has discovered that birds of a feather flock together. Perhaps you conducted business transactions with a person or party who is currently being audited by the IRS. And then *you* get audited. It doesn't seem fair, but…life isn't fair. Related party audits happen

Computer DIF & UI DIF scores – A closely-guarded secret computer algorithm that was originally developed in the mid-20th century is used regularly by the IRS. They use it to determine any number of different items on your tax return that seem to fall outside of their "normal range" of scores. These scores could relate to how the numbers on your tax return factor into their secret algorithm. Or how they factor into the type of tax return you filed in a tax year. Nobody knows. What we do know is that the higher the DIF score, the greater the likelihood a return will be selected for audit. Another type of score is the UI DIF score. It is based on a probability that income was not reported on a specific type of tax return. Again, nobody knows the formula, but we know the formula exists.

Random selection – This type of audit is a popular urban myth, like sightings of the Loch Ness Monster. In my years of experience representing individuals and small businesses before the IRS, I have never seen a random audit.

 An audit always begins for a reason– typically multiple reasons -- unless you prefer to ignore the man hiding behind the curtain, wearing dark sunglasses and a heavy black overcoat.

You tap him on the shoulder to ask him if he knows *why you.* The man removes his dark sunglasses and says, *"Don't you mean how? I mean, do you know how?"*

HOW Am I Being Audited?

 **What are the different types of IRS audits?**

The types of returns that the IRS selects for audit and the different methods of conducting an audit are numerous. Each type of income tax audit for individual taxpayers has specific characteristics and traits. Knowing **how** you are being audited will help you determine **what** documents you need, **where** to send them, and whether you need to enlist the help of a tax professional.

 IRS Publication 3498, available via the IRS website or found by performing an internet search for "Pub 3498," is an additional resource document that provides a brief overview of the different type of audits.

Although income tax audits come in five primary varieties, this book discusses only four types of audits. State Department of Revenue are out of the range and scope of this book. The four types of IRS audits reviewed in the pages that follow are:

1. Correspondence Audits,
2. Office Audits,
3. Field Audits, And
4. Root Canal-Flavored (NRP) Audits.

Correspondence Audit

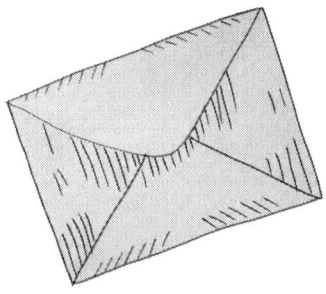

A Correspondence Audit is the most basic type of audit. This is generally how it goes: a letter is automatically and systematically generated by the IRS computer because an information document submitted to the IRS by someone else doesn't match up with the information that you reported on your tax return. It could be that you made a mistake while preparing a tax return. This could be as innocent as having your fingers on the wrong line of keys on a 10-key and mistakenly entering $153 instead of $486.

The letter the IRS sends begins by asserting that the Truly Troubled Taxpayer, Mr. Cliff Hanger in our example, must respond to this letter by a specific date and is commonly conducted entirely via USPS Mail, hence the name, correspondence audit.

 Typically, I have found that the IRS has not invested as much technical education into the personnel in charge of processing through correspondence audits.

You might even say that these employees have received very little in-depth training. However, just like the rest of us, they are human. Individuals who help our society move forward in a specific way that involves our nation's finances can sometimes simply make mistakes.

For this reason, always make sure to check and double-check every adjustment in IRS examiner's reports in a correspondence audit.

 Also make sure before proceeding to represent yourself in this type of audit that you are aware of how to exercise all of your rights as a taxpayer during a correspondence audit *(See Appendix A)*.

Office Audit

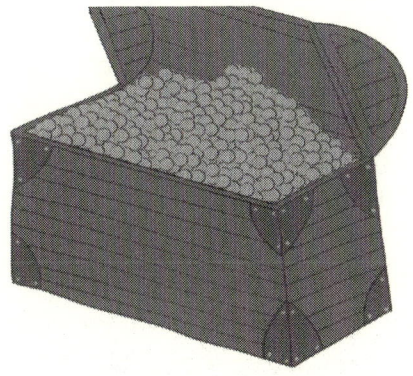

An <u>office audit</u> is more complicated than a correspondence audit. The Truly Troubled Taxpayer who is in an office audit is actually required to physically appear in an IRS office. The best scenario might include Mr. Hanger arriving at the IRS office with a copy of the tax return under examination along with all of the supporting documents Cliff relied upon to prepare the return in hand. In an office audit, the <u>IRS Tax Compliance Officer</u> is charged with examining specific line items that you have put on your tax return. An office audit might be the result of some deductions taken on a tax return that are grossly disproportionate in relation to the reported level of income. These tax deductions could be reported on a number of different tax forms, such as:

- ***Schedule C*** –is used to report income from self-employment in a specific line of business;

- *Schedule E* – This is where income from rental real estate properties, royalties, partnership or S-Corporation income, or from estates or trusts is reported to the IRS;
- *Form 2106* – This is where your deductions for unreimbursed Employee Business Expenses are reported;
- *Schedule A* – Personal, itemized deductions such as medical expenses or charitable deductions are commonly found here;
- *Schedule B* – Interest or dividend income is reported;
- *Schedule D* – is used to report capital gains or losses resulting from the sale of an asset, investment or a series of investments in an investment account.

The above list could go on, but it at least gives you an idea of some of the forms that could raise a red flag for an office audit. The first three forms (Schedules C, E, and 2106) have to do with reporting information for business purposes, and the last three forms (Schedules A, B, and D) are Forms used to report information for individual income and expenses.

 My experience for a typical office audit has shown that the examiner plans on the face-to-face interview concluding within a two- to four-hour period.

The examiner might have budgeted up to 45 minutes of that time to ask you a barrage of personal, get-to-know-you questions. These easy to understand questions are usually quite unanticipated. This method of conducting the interview enables the examiner to control the interview to their advantage. You should keep this in mind and try to make the most of this short span of time to *your* advantage.

The primary purpose of this level of interviewing is to make sure that YOU are YOU and that the examiner leaves no rock unturned. The purpose of looking under every rock and asking very detailed questions about some seemingly mundane topics is to ensure that they are doing their job as per Internal Revenue Manual 4.10.3.3.

 They are in search of unreported income.

Did you report all items of income on your tax return? Have you received any inheritances in the year under audit? Do you have any cash, money, or treasure chests filled with gold doubloons buried in your back yard?

At this stage of the interview, subtle nuances in communicating with the examiner can quickly transform anyone into a Truly Troubled Taxpayer. Remember: their job is to ensure that you reported the correct amount of income so they can calculate the proper amount of tax. Nothing technical about the language used, but ensuring that they calculate the proper amount of tax is what they are to determine (with your help, of course).

 Having a disinterested 3rd party represent you can significantly be to your advantage, and it could be the best opportunity you have of gliding through this type of audit.

Field Audit

 *Specific IRS examiner audit techniques*
What to do if you need help in your audit

If you are the subject of an IRS field audit, the best advice I can offer is immediately hire a professional to represent you. My reason for making this recommendation is simple. An IRS Revenue Agent (RA) legitimately expects you to be present while they inspect your place of business and conduct the audit in person. A field audit might cover a similar range of topics as an office audit, but a field audit often involves a much deeper scope of investigation in addition to demanding a great deal more time to complete. And rather than inviting you to visit their office location, the IRS often expects to pay you a visit at your home or place of business.

One of the initial purposes of a field audit might be to confirm whether you are or are not actually conducting a legitimate business, to examine and inspect your place of work, and review all of your business processes and record keeping. IRS examiners may use one of the many Audit Techniques Guides (ATGs) or Market Segment Specialization Program (MSSPs) to assist them in preparing a series of questions to ask you for the audit. A field audit can last as long as 6-18 months.

 If you don't have anything better to do on an evening or a weekend, you can do an internet search on "IRS ATG," and you'll get an idea of what I mean.

Especially in this type of audit, the IRS Revenue Agent can seem like a friendly person. However, their outward appearance is being used to soothe you into volunteering more information than what is necessary. This information will gradually be used against you as you paint yourself into a corner like Bob Ross, the artist who used to share his joy of painting on PBS.

National Research Project (NRP) Audit

Even more traumatic that a field audit is something called a National Research Project Audit (NRP); the closest thing in the world to a random audit. The IRS examiner is charged with examining each number on every line item on your tax return, a line-by-line audit from "H-E-double hockey sticks." That means every dollar amount you entered on your tax return could be suspect to further investigation. Root canal performed by the IRS. The occurrence of this type of audit has been extremely rare. In my practice, I have noticed an increase over the past few years. In addition, I have received the assurance from a couple of Revenue Agents that we can anticipate seeing more NRP audits in the future.

 For either a field audit or an NRP audit, I highly recommended that you engage the services of a credentialed tax professional (i.e. Enrolled Agent) to represent you in the audit.

Now that the four types of audits have been introduced and briefly reviewed, it is time to revisit the Mr. Cliff Hanger. While at the coffee shop, he overheard that Enrolled Agents are America's Tax Experts, federally-licensed tax practitioners who can represent taxpayers before the IRS when it comes to collections, audits and appeals. Cliff wanted to know how to select the most qualified Enrolled Agent. A friend from his work mentioned how extremely satisfying it was to work with an NTPI Fellow®.

NTPI Fellows are individuals who exceed the IRS's minimum standard for continuing education and are dedicated to staying on top of the latest changes to the US Tax Code.

The process of becoming an NTPI Fellow® takes several years. NTPI Fellows have completed a program of study that covers all facets of representing clients before the IRS. They have learned to guide their clients through the treacherous maze known as the IRS. NTPI Fellows have studied a broad range of topics to help resolve their client's tax issues, including:

- How to communicate with the IRS at various levels in the organization;
- How to assist taxpayers who haven't filed their taxes for some time;
- How to prepare taxpayers currently going through an IRS audit;
- How to represent taxpayers through the IRS Office of Appeals process and how to communicate with appeals officers;

- Various aspects of tax research and the best resources to rely upon;
- The collections division of the IRS;
- <u>Innocent spouse</u> considerations;
- How to process an Freedom of Information Act request to obtain your records from the IRS.

The list could go on, but this should give you a good idea that an NTPI Fellow is the best-qualified tax professional to help you resolve your tax issue. When looking for an Enrolled Agent to represent you before the IRS at <u>http://taxexperts.naea.org/</u> remember to ask them if they are an NTPI Fellow®.

Organize Your Documents

 *How to best prepare documents for an audit*

Once you have a greater understanding of the possible reason(s)

1. why you're being audited and
2. what type of IRS audit you may be forced to deal with,

you can start going through your records. Your next objective is to find the relevant receipts and documents that you relied upon to arrive at the numbers you entered when you prepared your income tax return.

 A gentle reminder: Never, under any circumstances – never – ever – send in your original documents (or your only copy of a document) to the IRS.

If you cannot find a document that the IRS examiner is requesting, immediately get a copy from the source or issuer of the original document(s). Make the examiner aware of the fact that you have posted requests and are waiting for additional documents to arrive. Time is not on your side in this type of an IRS audit. Cooperating with the examiner to the fullest extent possible and complying with all the requests from the IRS will make all the difference in the world.

When you explain your records are missing or you lost them in a move across the country, IRS Examiners do not pause progressing through the audit. Not only will they not accept your excuse, the examiner will also disallow your deduction until you are able to produce support for the positions you took on your tax return. Disallowed deductions tend to snowball, creating additional taxable income on your tax return, which translates into a bigger tax bill.

Your documentation is everything to the Revenue Agent. Their precise attention to detail is what sets them apart from other IRS tax researchers. The examiner's job is to study your records and apply their interpretation of the current tax law as it pertains to your tax return. Their focus can seem to be very narrow. To expand their vision of reality, you can explain the circumstances of your particular individual situation and be prepared to provide proof (which translates into a doctor's letter of the actual x-ray images of your broken hip).

 It seems to me that IRS examiners act as if they were trained in boot camp to not regard taxpayers as being worthy of much trust. This particular attribute adds fuel to their very narrow focus.

The topic of document organization could on its own fill an entire book. This book covers a few of the topics related to document organization in a couple of chapters. This is largely due to the immense breadth of information the IRS can request with Form 4564, an Information Document Request (IDR). For the purposes of this book, focus on the overall process and realize that you must neatly organize your documents. However, it may not be realistic for you to have assembled all the information the examiner requested as quickly as was required.

If you do not have all the information requested, be sure to contact the examiner assigned to your audit to discuss what information you currently have ready. You can find their phone number in the audit notification letter that the IRS initially sent out to you. It may be possible to begin your audit with the supplement of information currently available to you rather than postponing your appointment. The quicker the audit begins, the quicker you can reach a resolution with the IRS. With expedience and swiftness in mind, remember that if your rescheduled appointment is beyond 45 days from the date on the initial letter you received, you examiner requires getting a group manager's approval to reschedule your appointment.

 Read that last sentence again. Did you see that? You might be able to reschedule your appointment!

Cliff Hanger used this opportunity to request more time before the time came for the face-to-face tax audit and went old school. Cliff pulled out a blank sheet of paper and laid the letter from the IRS right beside of it for easy reference. He wanted to do this right. For starters, The Cliff wanted to be able to address the IRS employee by *First and Last Name, with the proper IRS Title.*

Sample Letter to Reschedule

Dear *Examiner's First & Last Name, IRS Title*

Due to unforeseen circumstances beyond my control, it has become necessary for me to submit a request to reschedule my tax audit appointment that was scheduled for (*Day, Date, Month, and Year*).

(Use at least the entire second paragraph to list the gory details of all your extenuating circumstances. Below is an example)

Two weeks ago, my daughter broke her left leg in a dance competition at school, and I had to take some time off work. I have been spoon-feeding her chicken noodle soup and helping her with her schoolwork at home. Last night I felt so tired my eyes were droopy carrying all her schoolbooks as I walked down the stairs. I tried to step over my toddler son's firetruck, but the books were too heavy. I twisted and sprained my ankle before I tumbled down 3 steps, landed on my chin and broke a crown on one of my front teeth. I am currently on pain medication and am waiting to get in to see an endodontist to get my tooth fixed.

I will be in touch with you so that we can schedule another date for my appointment within the next 10 business days. (By making this kind of promise to contact the examiner, you give them more assurance that you will follow through as soon as you are able.)

(*Do not use the following sentence if it does not apply*) I am certain that I have collected all my documents and they are complete. I can assure you that there will be no more delays. If your group manager requires you to contact me sooner, please leave me a voicemail at *(xxx) xxx-xxxx*. I will reply as soon as I am able.

Sincerely,

Mr. C. Hanger

Types Of Documents Requested

 *How to best prepare documents*

Although it is possible to postpone your audit, eventually you will have to meet face-to-face with the examiner. You will typically have a very short window of time to get your paperwork in order once the date for your audit is finally scheduled. The letter you received from the IRS should include a detailed listing of all the areas of your return the auditor expects to examine along with some documents to support the numbers you reported on your tax return. Some of these documents may include:

- W-2s,
- 1099s,
- Bank statements, both personal and business,
- Additional proofs of income,
- Financial investment account statements,
- Bills, receipts, or other proof of expenses incurred, such as meals & entertainment, travel, or a mileage log.

 The IRS prefers paper copies of your documentation but remember to send <u>copies</u> – do not provide the only copy or original source document.

The IRS has a pilot program that allows for electronic submission of certain records. This program is on an invitation-only status, however. Check with the examiner assigned to your audit to determine what is appropriate for your particular audit.

It is important to make a distinction between personal and business expenses. Generally, taxpayers like Cliff cannot deduct personal, living, or family expenses (IRC § 262). However, if there is an expense for something that was partly for business and partly for personal purposes, the business portion qualifies as a deduction. The total percentage of business use must be determined in order to calculate the business expense (deductible) and the personal portion (non-deductible).

Business expenses are little more complicated. The thought came to me: how do I fit a ton of content into this book and keep it concise? I pick my topics wisely. I have chosen to address the hot topic tax deductions that are most commonly challenged in an IRS audit. I have divided them in terms of where these expenses are reported as a deduction on an income tax return. As mentioned previously,

Schedule C is the form used to report income from self-employment in a specific line of business. I address schedule C deductions in depth.

Before I begin with deductions contested on Schedule C, a few terms and topics deserve clarification.

The Three P's

For each expense or deduction contested by the IRS in the audit of an income tax return, at least three layers of a financial transaction must be presented to the IRS in order to prove the deduction is legitimate. First, the three P's.

- Proof of **Purchase**
- Proof of **Payment**
- Proof of **Purpose**

If the IRS is questioning business travel deductions, for example, the proof of payment, like a credit card statement for a hotel bill, will not be enough. In order to prove that all expenses were legitimate deductions, the receipt from the hotel (proof of purchase) is seen as evidence to the IRS that the allowable expenses actually took place. Missing is the third P, proof of an actual business purpose.

A part of proof of purpose is showing that these expenses were both <u>ordinary and necessary</u>. The amount paid to the hotel that was for overnight lodging might be an acceptable deduction if staying overnight from time to time is both an **ordinary** activity in a particular line of business and a **necessary** expense in order to produce income. However, the amount paid for a round of drinks at the hotel bar is not an expense that the IRS sees as ordinary in the course of business and nor is it a necessary expense to produce income. This charge would not show up separately on a credit card statement (proof of payment), but it would show up on an itemized hotel receipt (proof of purchase). Regardless of whether or not there is a proof of purchase (receipt) and proof of payment (bank or credit card statement); there is still a lack of proof of a legitimate business purpose for the drinks.

Congress drafted things a certain way for multiple reasons. The Internal Revenue Code does not allow unlimited deductions for all the operating expenses paid in the course of business. However, IRC § 162 allows deductions for **ordinary and necessary** trade or business expenses paid or incurred during the course of a taxable year. Although the IRC uses the terms **"ordinary"** and **"necessary,"** these terms are not defined anywhere in the Internal Revenue Code..

 IRC § 162 reads: *"In general There shall be allowed as a deduction all the* **ordinary** *and* **necessary** *expenses paid or incurred during the taxable year in carrying on any trade or business, including--"* (**bold** text added for emphasis).

In a landmark case entitled Welch v. Helvering (**Welch v. Helvering, 290 U.S. 111 (1933),** the Supreme Court stated that the words **"ordinary"** and **"necessary"** have different meanings. The definitions for both **"ordinary"** and **"necessary"** must be satisfied for business owners to take an expense as a deduction. The Supreme Court described an **"ordinary"** expense as **customary** or **usual** and **of common or frequent occurrence** in the taxpayer's trade or business.

The Court describes a **"necessary"** expense as one that is **appropriate** and **helpful** for development of the business. The key words associated with the term necessary are **convenient**, *useful*, **essential**, **appropriate**, and **helpful**. In Publication 535, the IRS summarizes the findings and opinions of their interpretations of the terms **ordinary** and **necessary.** The intent is to help the Truly Troubled Taxpayers understand what the IRS regards as legitimate business expenses. In order to be deductible, expenses must meet the requirements for both **ordinary** and **necessary**. Obviously, the facts and circumstances and the intention of the

Truly Troubled Taxpayer will prevail over any absolute standard, but this gives a better understanding of the terms **"ordinary"** and **"necessary"** as they pertain to an audit.

Business Expenses - Schedule C

Business expenses are the cost of carrying on a trade or business. These expenses are usually deductible if the business operates to make a profit in three out of every five years.

Car & Truck Expenses

As per **IRC § 162** - A copy of a vehicle mileage log for each tax year would help substantiate (prove) this deduction. A vehicle mileage log can be kept in the glovebox and updated throughout the year to track the business miles traveled. The following four or five criteria need to be resident on a vehicle mileage log for the business miles traveled: the date of the business miles traveled, the destination of the business miles traveled, the business purpose of the business miles traveled and the beginning and ending odometer reading for the date of the business miles traveled. An alternative to beginning and ending odometer readings is recording the total miles traveled for each record of business miles traveled. Cliff Hanger, for example, commonly used an Excel Spreadsheet to compile a vehicle mileage log.

Additionally, Cliff needed to provide proof that his primary residence (home) was his principal place of business. This can be in the form of a hand-drawn sketch of the home with an indication of the area that Cliff used exclusively for conducting business. Accompanying this information with photographs of Cliff's home office would also be helpful. Taxpayers frequently forget to take the Business Use of Home deduction on form 8829 of their income tax return (covered later on page 59). The IRS can legitimately have a skeptical view of vehicle mileage logs presented, and will likely disallow these deductions if a taxpayer like Cliff is unable to show that his principal place of business is his home.

Travel - IRC § 162

(IRC = Internal Revenue Code, the "Code") IRC § 162 allows deductions for ordinary and necessary trade or **business** expenses that took place in a tax year. Specifically spelled out, IRC § 162(a) reads:

*"In general There shall be allowed as a deduction all the **ordinary** and **necessary** expenses paid or incurred during the taxable year in carrying on any trade or business, including traveling expenses (including amounts expended*

for meals and lodging other than amounts which are lavish or extravagant under the circumstances) while away from home in the pursuit of a trade or business... (**bold** text added for emphasis).

Travel expenses were in the example on page 40. Did you see *including amounts expended for meals* mentioned above? The deduction for meals under this code section is limited to "*while away from home in the pursuit of a trade or business.*" That means a Mr. Hanger has to be away from his "tax home" overnight. That means away from where Cliff does business. There is a specific code section that deals with meals and entertainment, IRC § 274(d).

Meals & Entertainment - IRC § 274(d)

This section of the Internal Revenue Code begins by expressly dis-allowing any type of entertainment expense.

"In General, no deduction shall be allowed for any item of entertainment, amusement, or recreation...unless the taxpayer substantiates by adequate records or by sufficient evidence..."

These expenses for meals and entertainment need to be business related, and two of the four records required to prove these purchases can be as simple as saving your receipts:

- the **amount** of the meal or entertainment expense can easily be found on the receipt,

- the **time, date and place** of the meal or entertainment expense should appear on the printed receipt,

- the **business purpose** – this information would be handwritten contemporaneously on each receipt. That means a Cliff needs to be getting some business done with a client or prospective client. Finally,

- the **business relationship** with the client or business contact being entertained would also need to be contemporaneously handwritten on each receipt.

Contemporaneously just means at the same time as the meal or entertainment expense occurred. This could be the evening of or the day after the entertainment occurred. It could also mean a week later. It intentionally does **not** mean that this type of record keeping can take place right after a Cliff gets an audit notification from the IRS. This stack of receipts needs to be totaled up to make it easier for the examiner to do their job. It could help if Cliff arrange the receipts in chronological order, but that is not entirely necessary as long as the receipts are all totaled up in the same order the receipts are stacked. That way the examiner could very easily take a sampling of the expenses and move on to another area.

Proof of payment means including a credit card and/or bank statement with the associated purchases highlighted.

Utilities - IRC § 162

If Cliff happens to have a separate office away from home and the utility expense is the directly related to the business, expenses claimed as a deduction can be the telephone bill, the gas bill, the electric bill, and the water/sewer bill. Cliff would need to obtain receipts for all twelve months of each utility expense. This means a stack of 12 monthly telephone receipts, a stack of 12 monthly lights receipts, a stack of 12 monthly gas receipts, a stack of 12 monthly electricity receipts, and a stack of 12 monthly water/sewer receipts. To finish things off, include an Excel spreadsheet totaling up the entire stack of utility receipts in chronological order on top. Proof of payment will be satisfied by highlighting the bank statement in a different color for each utility bill paid for all 12 months of the year. The expenses of utilities as discussed here are only for businesses -- not personal expenses for home utilities. Listing home office utility expenses here is a common mistake in self-prepared tax returns. Home Office is covered later on page 56.

Legal And Professional - IRC § 162

Fees charged for preparing Schedules C, C-EZ, SE, 4562, 8829, and accompanying worksheets are deductible as ordinary and necessary expenses directly related to operating a business. Other business professional services like payroll, accounting, and lawyer's fees may also considered deductions under the banner of Legal and Professional expenses. These types of deductions need the 3 Ps, which includes all receipts for proof of purchase, with a sheet totaling them up on top. Highlighted payments on a bank or credit card statement will suffice for proof of payment. Proof of a business purpose can be an explanatory page relating each specific expense to a purpose that is both ordinary and necessary.

Supplies - IRC § 162

The cost of supplies required to create or produce a product or service are deductible. Once created however, the product becomes inventory. Cliff Hanger needs to count the inventory and record it at the beginning and end of each year, but inventory is not deductible. Deductions for supplies still need to be supported by the 3 Ps. Each purchase for supplies requires a receipt for proof of purchase, and a sheet totaling up the receipts. Contact the bank or credit card company in order to get a statement to highlight these expenses to satisfy proof payment. Depending on the line of business, an explanatory page informing the examiner of how each type of supplies purchased relates to a specific ordinary and necessary business purpose. Remember to lay an Excel spreadsheet or 10-key tape totaling up all of the receipts on top of the pile of receipts.

Cost Of Goods Sold - IRC § 162

Raw materials and supplies purchased for manufacturing a product can be deducted as cost of goods sold. Some expenses of delivering a service may also be included in figuring the cost of goods sold. If an expense is included in the cost of goods sold, the same expense cannot be taken as a deduction again as a business expense.

The shorthand for this type of taking a deduction twice is "double-dipping." Picture a social gathering where the person in front of your friend dips a carrot into ranch sauce, takes a bite, and then dips the carrot into the ranch sauce again. Eww! No "double-dipping" is allowed when taking tax deductions.

The following are types of expenses that go into figuring the cost of goods sold.

- The cost of products or raw materials,
- The cost of transporting products, and
- The cost of storing products.

The direct cost of labor for workers who produce a product or deliver a service is deductible; – this deduction could also include employer contributions to an employer-sponsored retirement plan.

All receipts for each purchase of a COGS item needs to be produced and have the actual expense highlighted on the receipt to satisfy the proof of purchase. An Excel spreadsheet or 10-key tape totaling up all of the receipts should rest on top of the pile of receipts, like a fax cover sheet. Satisfy proof of payment by highlighting the purchase transaction on a bank or credit card statement. Finally, depending on the types of materials that go into producing a product or service, a brief description explaining of how each purchase relates to a specific ordinary and necessary business purpose.

Insurance

Generally, the ordinary and necessary cost of insurance is a business expense if it is for a trade, business, or profession. A quick review of some kinds of insurance that may qualify as a deduction:

- Fire, theft, or flood (or a similar type of insurance);
- Credit insurance that covers losses from unpaid business (bad debt);
- Group hospitalization and medical insurance for employees, which could include long-term care insurance;
- Liability insurance for your line of business;
- Insurance that covers a business against personal liability for professional negligence resulting in injury or damage to patients or clients;
- Workers' compensation insurance that covers a business against claims for bodily injuries or job-related diseases suffered by employees;
- Life insurance covering employees (if the Truly Troubled Taxpayer is not listed as the beneficiary);
- Business interruption insurance that pays for lost profits in the event of a business shut down; and

- Contributions to state unemployment insurance are deductible as taxes;

If you use the standard mileage rate to figure your deductible car expenses, deducting direct expenses like car insurance premiums is actually double-dipping. As mentioned before, no double-dipping is allowed. You can deduct mileage or actual expenses, not both.

However, car, truck, and other vehicle insurance that covers vehicles used in business for liability, damages, and other losses does qualify as a deduction. If a vehicle is split between business and personal use, only the part of the insurance premium that applies to the business use of the vehicle is deductible.

The following insurance expenses do not qualify as a deduction:

- amounts credited to a reserve set up for self-insurance,
- premiums for a policy that pays for lost earnings due to sickness/disability,
- personal life insurance and annuities, or
- Insurance used to secure a loan.

Proof of purchase requires producing an entire copy of all insurance policies – not just the declarations page. This policy will probably be the equivalent of a receipt, showing the cost of insurance. Highlighting the payments made on a bank or credit card statement takes care of proof of payment. Any insurance expensed and deducted needs to have a specific ordinary and necessary business purpose, which will depend on the type of business and the type of insurance.

Repairs & Maintenance

Something broke and needed repair. Determining whether the ordinary and necessary cost of a repair should be expensed as a repair or capitalized and depreciated is a bit more complex. In the *Repairs* section of Publication 535, the IRS clarifies the distinction between maintenance and repairs:

"The cost of repairing or improving property used in your trade or business is either a deductible (expense) or (a) capital expense."

That means some types of repairs are deductible in the current tax year as a deductible expense. Some other types of repairs require adding the cost of the repair to the cost of another asset and depreciating the cost of the repair over several years as a capital expense. In many cases, this means it will take several years to deduct the actual cost of some types of repairs.

A pile of the actual receipts with a cover sheet totaling them all up is good for starters (and substantiating proof of purchase). The same expenses highlighted on a credit card or bank statement should be enough to fulfill the requirements of proof of payment. Proof of business purpose requires illustrating to the examiner a purpose that is both ordinary in the course of business and necessary to generate a profit.

Interest-Other

Business interest expense is an amount charged for the use of money borrowed for business activities. Cliff cannot deduct the entire amount of a loan unless in the same taxable year Mr. Hanger repaid the loan. The original loan documents would substantiate the proof of purchase. If Cliff highlights the monthly payments on a bank statement, then would help, but the only deductible expenses allowed is the interest. An end-of-year bank statement would do all the heavy lifting to satisfy the proof of payment requirement. A loan taken out for a personal purpose would not satisfy then the proof of an ordinary and necessary business purpose. The interest on a loan secured by a business asset used in the course of business would, however.

Rent or Lease

When shown to be ordinary and necessary in the course of doing business, the cost of renting or leasing a vehicle, machinery, equipment, office space, or storage space can be substantiated to the examiner. The rental or lease agreement would prove the purchase actually took place. A highlighted credit card or bank statement would prove the monthly payments. Whether or not the rental expense was an ordinary and necessary business purpose depends on the nature of the Cliff's or any other taxpayer's line of business. A written, detailed description of how the renal or lease expense relates to a taxpayer's line of business could satisfy this requirement for the examiner during the audit.

Office Expenses

The ordinary and necessary business expenses that relate to office expenses includes folders, paper and paper clips, staples and staplers, pens and pencils, coffee for clients, a computer, a printer, toner for the printer, a filing cabinet, and so on and so forth. Receipts? Proof of purchase - check! Sheet totaling up all of the receipts? Proof of payment - check! Ordinary and necessary business purpose? Proof of purpose - check! Ya gotta love checklists for their efficiency!

Business Use Of Home

Utilities costs are either personal (nondeductible) or business use (deductible). If Cliff sets aside a part of his home and uses that space exclusively for business purposes, some expenses may qualify as a deduction for the business use of home. These expenses include mortgage interest, property taxes, homeowner's insurance, repairs made to the home, depreciation, and a fractional portion of all 12 months of all utilities bills paid (electric, gas, telephone, waste disposal, water & sewer).

For the purpose of illustration, say the amount of square footage the home office takes up is 100 square feet. Whatever that amount comes out to, it is divided by total finished square footage of the home (1500 square feet, for example) to arrive at a fraction (1/15 or 6.67% in this example).

Multiply all 12 months of each expense by this percentage to determine the deductible portion of each expense and then add them all up. This is the amount allowed for the business use of home deduction.

Proof of purchase includes the mortgage interest statement (form 1098), which, if escrowed, could include a portion of the annual payment property tax paid and the homeowner's insurance. If the property taxes and homeowner's insurance payments were not paid along with the mortgage payment, the actual property tax statement from the county would need to be produced for proof of purchase and a credit card or bank statement to show that the tax has been paid for proof of payment.

Proof of purchase for repairs requires a bill of sale for each repair that could include labor and materials. If repairs were paid for in cash, the actual bill of sale should include that as well for proof of payment. Usually a Mr. Cliff Hanger would illustrate proof of payment for repairs with a bank statement or credit card statement.

Proof of purchase also includes obtaining receipts for all twelve months of all five utilities, totaling up each type of utility expense on a cover sheet and totaling all of the utility expenses together. Taxpayers like Cliff can show proof of payment by adequately highlighting each specific payment made on a bank or credit card or bank statement. It usually works out best if each utility is assigned to a different colored highlighter and a color-code key is drawn on the front sheet of the bank or credit card statement.

Other Schedule C expenses requiring substantiation include:

- Advertising
- Commission & Fees – may require 1096 & 1099s

- Contract Labor- requires 1096 & 1099s
- Self-Employed Health Insurance
- Taxes & Licenses
- Wages

These areas all require the 3Ps: proof of purchase consisting of receipts, proof of payment consisting of properly marked-up bank or credit card statements, and a legitimate proof of business purpose that is both ordinary and necessary.

Organization is Key!

How to best organize documents for an audit

Once you have all of the copies of your original materials assembled, it is a good idea to get them organized -- especially if you are going into a face-to-face audit. Good organization shows the examiner that you are a responsible taxpayer, and it may help in limiting the scope of the IRS investigation. The order in which the information was requested on the Information Document Request (or IDR, Form 4564 – see *Appendix B*) is a good starting point for assembling your documents.

Cliff really had his things organized! Evidence for each topic on the Information Document Request had been printed, and 3-hole punched, labeled with a post-it tab sticking out and assembled in a very specific order in a 3-ring binder with a table of contents when arriving at the Internal Revenue Service Center. Cliff was ready for anything…but what if the examiner didn't ask questions in the right order?

The Face-to-Face Audit

 *Specific techniques the IRS uses in an audit*

Keep in mind that the examiner will determine the direction and the speed of processing through the audit. As former IRS trial attorney Howard Levy pointed out, *"When your head is in the mouth of the bear, say 'nice bear.' It's that simple."* Be ready to go in whatever direction the examiner chooses to direct your attention. Sometimes the examiner proceeds in sequential order, and sometimes an examiner goes for the low hanging fruit. If a single line item on your tax return can substantially change in the amount of taxable income you reported on your income tax return, it's as easy to grab a piece of fruit that hangs low enough on the branch for an IRS examiner with shorter legs to reach. More plainly, sometimes the examiner will go for the easy cash first and then deal with the rest of the items that the computer or selection group picked for the audit in whatever order is more convenient to the auditor. The technical terms are professional skepticism, and presuming you are neither honest nor dishonest. They've got a job to do, and it's an understatement to say that many examiners do a very good job at what they do best.

In an office audit, the IRS routinely asks about some information that did not appear in the initial IDR.

IRS Tax Compliance Officers and Agents are trained and highly skilled at obtaining additional information from Truly Troubled Taxpayers. This is one example of one of the many risks in a face-to-face audit. IRS audit examiners are among the best at not making you feel threatened.

Many times, however, taxpayers will make the mistake of offering too much information in answering a question during the face-to-face interview.

During the face-to-face audit examination, the IRS has a playbook, and you should be aware of the rules of the game they play. It is the Internal Revenue Manual or IRM for short. It is their bible.

It has all kinds of tasty tidbits of tactics they use and instructions on how to extract information from taxpayers. The IRS then sends examiners away to the most remote locations on planet earth. These places are where examiners sit to receive specialized training and instruction in conducting different types of audits. By remote locations, I mean average cities within the contiguous United States where ordinary people conduct ordinary training. However, the IRS campus used for this training that most closely resembles the Death Star in size is the one in Kansas City and not the ones in Indianapolis or Saint Louis. It should be no surprise that most of the structure in Kansas City is buried deep underground, hidden from view.

 Examiners are specifically trained to use effective interview techniques.

In chapter 2 of the Pre-Audit & Effective Interview Techniques Guide, examiners are trained to *"use exact and precise questions requiring a direct reply and, if the taxpayer responds with evasive replies (pay attention to words, such as: because, perhaps, sometimes, maybe), immediately question such answers until you have obtained a complete, satisfactory answer."* To go deep on this, point on page 2-46, the bullet point *"During an interview, be alert to the possibility of misrepresentation by the interviewee,"* which was immediately followed by the statement, *"During an interview, be alert to the possibility of misrepresentation by the interviewee."* In case you fell asleep reading this, the IRS is on the lookout for taxpayers not telling the truth. This statement actually appears twice on the same page.

It is important to be honest and respond as thoroughly as you can, but be careful not to divulge information outside of the scope of the audit. Be prepared and be armed with the truth because IRS examiners are not pushovers.

 Remember: many of them traveled to IRS boot camp at the Kansas City Death Star at least once – twice if they qualify for special training!

I wonder what they learn there... Cliff Hanger wonders aloud.

Specific Interview Techniques

 *Specific audit techniques*

In the process of being trained as professional skeptics, some of the techniques learned by examiners in the Audit Technique Guide include:

1. Make eye contact.
2. Put the taxpayer at ease.
3. Read the taxpayer's non-verbal language (body language).
4. Be aware of the Examiner's non-verbal language.
5. Appear interested.
6. Control the interview.
7. Appear confident.

Does that sound at all like the 20th century sales techniques of a used car salesman?

The initial stage of the interview does not begin with asking you about your tax return. As was noted earlier, the questions begin with simple and direct questions about you, your family, your background, and your level of knowledge about the process of an audit. Does that make you feel more at ease?

- *The first question asked almost always is --Have you received Publication 1?*
- *Do you understand the audit process?*
- *Is the address on your tax return correct?*
- *What is your education level?*
- *What is your Spouse's education level?*
- *Where is your current place of employment?*
- *Have you ever been divorced?*
- *Has your wife been divorced?*
- *Do you have a safe deposit box?*
- *If yes, can you describe the contents?*
- *How much cash do you normally have on hand?*
- *Do you have a website you use for business?*
- *Do you participate in online gambling?*
- *Do you have any foreign bank accounts?*
- *Do you buy or sell things on eBay or Craigslist?*
- *Do you participate in online banking or bill paying?*
- *Have you received any inheritances, gifts, or loans?*
- *Do you engage in any bartering activities?*

And the questions go on and on for 45 minutes or longer – and then it's time to start asking questions about the items they have called into question regarding how you reported your income or expenses on the tax return under audit.

- Who maintains your books?
- Where did they learn bookkeeping?
- What percentage of your income comes from cash?
- What bank accounts are maintained?
- Do you deposit all of your income receipts? Who deposits it?
- What do you do if you get cash?
- How are personal withdrawals handled?

Regarding your income sources, do you have any income from:

- Interest
- Dividends
- Any Sale Of Assets
- Do you have any Other Jobs
- Any Investments
- Tips
- Commissions
- Do you have any income producing Hobbies
- Any income from Rent/Royalty
- Alimony
- A Partnership Or S Corporation
- Did you receive any Sick Pay
- Any Self-Employment Or Contract Labor
- Did you receive or pay out any Child Support
- Any Prizes Or Awards
- Bonuses
- Gambling or Lottery winnings
- Any Insurance
- Any income from any Estates or Trusts
- Did you get a State Tax Refund
- Any Employer Reimbursement
- Any Gifts or Inheritances that you received but do not report
- Any Scholarships; Fellowships; or Grants
- Any interest on or Loans Received
- Any Social Security income

- *Welfare*
- *Unemployment*
- *VA Benefits*
- *Military Allowance*
- *Do you have any Foreign Bank Accounts*
- *Any income from any Pensions*
- *Annuities*
- *Any Profit-Sharing, Keogh, or IRA Distributions*
- *Any Sale Of Stocks*
- *Any Foreign Income, Investments Or Transactions*
- *Amu Other income, and if so, please specify*
- *Could you please explain to me of any income that was received, but was not reported on your income tax return?*

 This line of questioning about your business affairs assists the examiner and not you at all.

The IRS suggests to their auditors to … *(technological pause)*…pause during office audits, encouraging taxpayers… *(Breathe in and hold it pause)*…such as yourself… *(Look down at papers pause)*…to fill in the… *(Make a checkmark and nod pause)*… silence with… *(Affirmative nod of the head with piercing eye contact pause)*… unintended disclosures. Don't fall for this trick. Their job is to trip you up and find some information that was inaccurately reported or misrepresented on your tax return. Be aware that when you volunteer irrelevant information to a tax examiner, no matter how innocent it may seem, it will be used against you later in the conversation. Do your best to answer the questions cautiously while at the same time making it appear as if you have no income to hide.

A Stressful Situation

After Cliff had reviewed all of the information requested by the IRS, the examination appeared to be very straightforward. The reality is that it is very difficult for any taxpayer to survive an IRS audit by handling the situation all alone. The examiner seemed to have a very narrow focus on things, and this created some limitations on what the IRS was able to take into consideration when processing Cliff's audit. It was as if the examiner had specifically selected the interview questions to use for Cliff's IRS audit. Each question seemed to fit his individual situation and circumstance in life. As a result, it was impossible for him to walk away from his IRS audit with zero changes made to his tax return.

This is because the IRS examiner's intention was to reveal and unravel Cliff's best defenses with this line of questioning. However, Cliff followed Rule #2. When answering questions, he kept his answers short & sweet, hesitating a little bit before answering each question. Cliff Hanger took some time to think about each question before he answered it. If he had not done so, the first time Cliff paused before giving his answer, the examiner might have thought that he could be trying to conceal the truth. Cliff had carefully constructed his responses to the IRS's inquiries so that they would provide direct answers to the examiner's specific questions and would not open the door for the examiner to peer into other parts of his tax return under audit – or tax returns from previous years.

However, this interviewing technique caused what normally would be a casual response by Cliff to a casual question asked by the IRS examiner into a response that was more emotional. The examiner wanted to ask Cliff a little bit more about that topic. His mild level of frustration or feeling of anxiety about something totally unrelated to the audit had the potential of having a more far-reaching financial impact than he had initially thought.

Audits are stressful and when people get nervous, people tend to talk too much. The IRS trains examiners to prompt you to speak and to listen closely to everything that comes out of your mouth. Talking too much is a very common mistake that has cost many a taxpayer lots of money in their IRS audit.

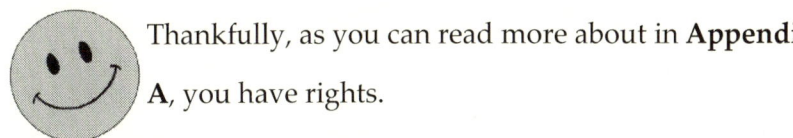 Thankfully, as you can read more about in **Appendix A**, you have rights.

Rule #1 – Anytime you feel uncomfortable, tell the examiner you choose representation and they are required to stop asking you questions. You have the right to be represented by a qualified tax professional when dealing with the IRS during an audit. Once you have done your research, sought representation, and retained the services of a qualified representative, you do not have to attend the audit in person. Your representative will appear in your place and speak on your behalf. The IRS cannot compel you to appear in person unless the examiner has a specific reason, produces the proof to his manager for approval and delivers a summons to your doorstep. More importantly, even if you the IRS sends you a summons to appear in person for your audit, you cannot be compelled to speak on your own behalf. Selecting a qualified representative has many benefits.

One of the many tremendous benefits of having an advocate like an Enrolled Agent (EA) represent you before the IRS is that it takes all the emotional drama out of the audit. The idea of having an Enrolled Agent assist and represent you throughout the entire examination process is brilliant, and you should probably take advantage of your right to representation.

Carefully Thought Out

 *What to do after the audit*

The audit was not quite over after the Cliff's grueling face-to-face examination. Once the initial interview with the IRS was complete, the examiner completely reviewed all of the documents and evidence that Mr. Hanger had provided in response to this audit.

The length of time it takes to complete this stage of the audit depends greatly on the type of audit you are in, how many audits the examiner has in their caseload, and how efficient the examiner is at processing through your audit material. The examiner will eventually mail you a report of the proposed adjustments and changes to your originally filed income tax return.

If you have any disagreements with the examiner during the audit, carefully write a letter of protest and request a conference with the examiner's direct supervisor or group manager. Handling everything at the lowest possible administrative level within the IRS is worth the extra effort because it has the potential of saving you more time and avoiding appeals.

Here are some alternatives available to you when you receive the initial report:

1. You can file a formal written protest with the examiner or file a written appeal to have a conference with the examiner's direct supervisor;
2. You can file a request for a Fast Track Mediation, where an appeals officer acts as a mediator between you and the IRS. Requesting an Appeals hearing, later on, is still on the table as an option if the eventual outcome of the Fast Track Mediation doesn't go the way you had hoped;
3. You can file a form 12202 with the IRS appeals division to request an independent review of your case by an appeals officer; or perhaps depending on the circumstances of what stage your audit is at, you might file a form 12153 to request a Collections Due Process (CDP) hearing; or
4. You can neglect the notice, wait 90 days, receive a <u>Notice of Deficiency (NOD)</u>, and file a **petition** with the US Tax Court without having to pay the proposed adjustment first.

At the end of an IRS audit, the IRS audit report asserts the amount owed. Although other avenues are available after Mr. Hanger received the final audit report, it is most important for him to understand the IRS audit report.

The Audit Report

 *Next steps after the face-to-face audit*

If the IRS finds that you owe them some tax, the examiner must follow some very specific protocols before the amount of tax you owe can be determined. Additionally, the IRS must follow their own guidelines in terms of how they notify you that you owe additional tax and how they propose to collect this tax from you.

The <u>Revenue Agent's Report (RAR)</u> or <u>Form 4549</u>, lists the changes the examiner proposes to make to your tax return. The

RAR is often accompanied by a "30-day letter" (letter 525) to notify you of your rights to an appeal and to begin counting down what is known as the 30-day clock.

In an ideal world, the IRS would only issue you an Audit Report with Form 4549 at the *end* of the audit. The reality is that IRS examiners have been known to issue a 4549 if taxpayers like Cliff Hanger fails to respond to the initial request the examiner sent out to request scheduling a face-to-face audit examination.

 The examiner is attempting to prompt Cliff to respond rather than pre-emptively closing the audit in favor of the IRS.

Failing to schedule a face-to-face audit examination with the IRS is tantamount to agreeing with all the adjustments in the report.

The issuance of the Form 4549 is not the end of the audit or the end of the world. However, when a Truly Troubled Taxpayer agrees with the IRS calculations and adjustments on the Form 4549, they should sign it and send it back via USPS certified return receipt to the address listed.

On the contrary, if Cliff does not agree that the audit was handled properly or feels that the facts do not support the examiner's adjustments, it is important to *not* sign the second page of the

Form 4549. This choice determines whether or not Cliff is able to challenge the IRS in Tax Court in the future on the issue currently under examination.

Sometimes a Truly Troubled Taxpayer does not agree with the adjustments proposed by the examiner and would like to know what all of the potential options are. This is a very good opportunity to consider locating and consulting with a tax professional with <u>unlimited practice rights</u> to represent taxpayers before the IRS, like an Enrolled Agent, CPA, or tax attorney.

Collection Due Process (CDP)

 *Next steps after the audit*
One of the doorways from audit into appeals

The Due Process Clause of the Fifth Amendment to the US Constitution provides that "no person...shall be...deprived of life, liberty, or property, without due process of law." Due process in this context requires you first be provided notice that you are about to be deprive and second that you have an opportunity for a hearing. The IRS must provide Cliff the following items of notice at the time the IRS issues a Collections Due Process (CDP) notice:

- **Publication 594**, The IRS Collection Process;
- **Publication 1660**, Collection Appeal Rights; and

- **Form 12153**, Request for a Collection Due Process or Equivalent Hearing.

If Cliff does not agree with the adjustments proposed by the examiner, they should file a written protest. This protest should contain the following: the facts and circumstances of the Cliff's position, the Internal Revenue Code references upon which the Cliff bases his position and analysis, and a conclusion of how this all pertains to the Cliff Hanger's audit. If the auditor does not agree and proposes a final adjustment, then before the examiner issues the 30-day letter request, the Mr. Hanger has the possibility of requesting a conference with the examiner's direct supervisor (or group manager).

 Taxpayers should take advantage of this opportunity. The chance that the group manager is going to alter the examiner's conclusions is remote and highly unlikely. However, all of the other opportunities available for Mr. Hanger at this point in the audit have very specific conditions, restrictions, and time constraints.

For example, if Cliff wants to appeal the IRS adjustments, he has 30 days to appeal the final decision of the IRS examination. This

30-day period begins with the mailing date of the RAR notice. The IRS is required to send every taxpayer a 30-day letter with the RAR that contains instructions on how to appeal the amount the IRS proposes.

Mr. Hanger may agree that the examiner's final audit report is correct. Alternatively, Cliff may disagree and find them in error. The report forms sent out in either case are virtually identical, except for the form names and numbers. Reports indicating you **agree** with the IRS include Form 4549, and reports indicating you **disagree** with the IRS include Form 886-A.

The only administrative level of appeals within the IRS is the local appeals office.

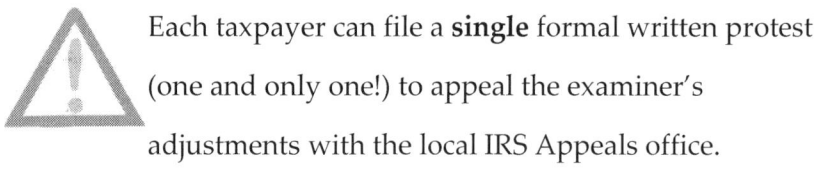

Each taxpayer can file a **single** formal written protest (one and only one!) to appeal the examiner's adjustments with the local IRS Appeals office.

This formal written protest will grant a single review of the IRS audit by an independent appeals officer who is impartial. By independent, I mean (*they mean*) that the appeals office is an agency independent of the IRS; independent from any IRS examination functions and all IRS collections functions. By impartial, I mean (*they mean*) that the appeals officer is impartial and disinterested in the eventual outcome of every specific hearing.

Depending upon the circumstances and outcome of the Cliff's particular audit, requesting an appeals hearing by filing a Form 12202 with your audit examiner may be a possibility.

 However, as I mentioned earlier in this book, everybody's tax situation is different.

If a Notice of Deficiency (NOD) accompanied the IRS audit report, things are a little different. Cliff might be able to appeal by filing a Form 12153, Request For A <u>Collection Due Process Hearing</u>. He needs to send this form to the address shown on the notice within 30 days from the date at the top of this letter.

If the Cliff does not file the original CDP request within the 30-day period as required by law, the IRS appeals office can grant an "equivalent" hearing. This hearing is essentially the same thing as the Collections Due Process (CDP) hearing, except for the fact that you will *never* effectively have the right to appeal the Notice of Determination (issued by the IRS Appeals Office) to the US Tax Court. That is why, in order to keep all options open, it is important to file the original Collections Due Process (CDP) request within the allotted 30-day period.

Meanwhile, Cliff had dozed off while reviewing the series of documents he had received from the IRS.

Beep! Beep! Beep! Beep!

Startled awake and thankful he had set the alarm, now he could really focus on – wait a minute! What time is it? Did he sleep past the deadline?

Deadlines - You Snooze, You Lose

If Mr. Cliff Hanger misses **any** of the deadlines prescribed by the IRS, he will find himself in IRS collections. As an IRS audit progresses, Cliff may find that missing IRS deadlines only makes the tax debt grow, become more painful and much more costly to resolve. Another strategy that speeds Cliff's path to being in IRS collections is not signing and returning notices that indicate agreement or disagreement with the IRS adjustments to the tax return under audit. When the 30-day period to respond to the 4549 expires, the IRS could eventually issue a letter that informs the Truly Troubled Taxpayer how absolutely the IRS is correct, usually referencing one of the many tax laws passed by Congress. This 90-day letter (a.k.a. statutory notice of deficiency, stat notice, or NOD) kindly explains the purpose of the notice they are sending, how much is owed to the IRS and what the options are.

 The burden to prove that the NOD is wrong (i.e. that you do not owe the IRS) rests on the shoulders of Mr. Cliff Hanger

The letter goes on to explain in detail:

1. How the IRS calculated Cliff's tax bill, and
2. What adjustments led to this calculation, i.e. the IRS has the authority to send this letter out under a law in the Internal Revenue Code known as IRC 6212(a)).

Beginning with the date on the notice, a 90-day window of time presented Cliff with a couple options:

1. He could agree now, or at any time during the 90-day window,
2. He could file a petition to have your case heard in Tax Court at any time during the 90-day window.

"Wait a minute! This is all starting to get a bit complicated and confusing!" the Cliff blurted out. "Can we back up a little bit? How did this all get started?"

How Did I Get Here?

Doorway from Audit to US Tax Court

Immediately before a trip to the emergency room resulting from a blow to the head at the mailbox, Mr. Cliff Hanger first got an IRS examiner's report of proposed changes to the tax return that he filed. In the examiner's report, the IRS proposed adjustments and the amount that Cliff owes them. Then a 30-day window of time opened up with which to agree or disagree with the conclusions that the IRS examiner copiously explained in the RAR. Cliff failed to respond to the 4549, the 30-day letter. He then received a 90-day letter, also known as a stat notice or a statutory Notice of Deficiency (NOD).

The cover letter sent with the Notice of Deficiency (NOD) explained how to contact the <u>Clerk of the U.S. Tax Court</u> for filing a Tax Court case. The cover letter did not mention this, but I will:

an NOD is one of only four "tickets" or "doorways" that will gain you access to having your case heard in Tax Court (IRC §§ 6212; 6213(b)).

A gentle reminder: keep track of all the deadlines associated with your tax controversy case because every one of them is extremely important.

If you miss any one of them (as they silently pop up and disappear), your options can become very limited very quickly. Failing to agree to the assessments or failing to timely file a petition with the U.S. Tax Court will result in the IRS rapidly assessing the tax and moving on to the next step of enforcing collecting your hard earned money.

It may appear to be the end of the audit, but this is not the end of Cliff Hanger's rights. The IRS examiner's findings are not final until the Cliff agrees or has exhausted all his administrative rights to appeal the examiner's conclusions with the IRS office of appeals, and through the United States Tax Court.

Cliff finished reading all of the documents and decided to disagree. The envelope from the IRS was not a peel-and-seal, so the glue on the back of the envelope left the residue of a sour and smoky taste with a plastic aftertaste in his mouth. Rubbing his tongue on the roof of his mouth to get rid of the flavor, Cliff began to wonder…*what is this appeals hearing thing all about?* He reached in his pocket for a stick of chewing gum. *What is the IRS office of appeals all about?*

Appeals

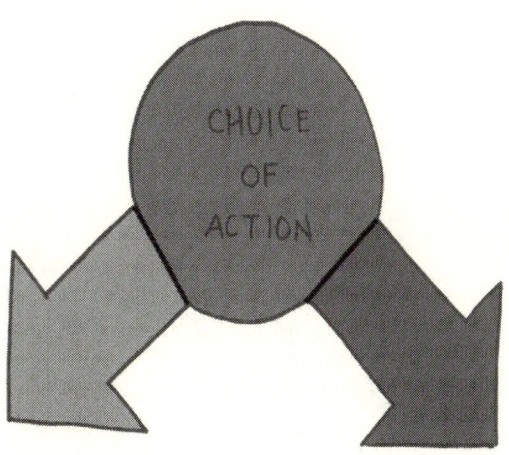

 *Next Steps after an audit
One of the doorways from Audit to Appeals*

The IRS Office of Appeals has the authority to hear most cases where taxpayers openly disagree with the IRS. The role of Appeals is to help resolve very specific types of disagreements taxpayers under audit might have with the IRS. The idea is to settle these disputes on a *fair* and *impartial basis* -- without going to court. By fair, they mean that the IRS Office of Appeals favors neither the government nor the taxpayer. This process of working through appeals is much more cost effective and less formal than immediately filing a petition to US Tax Court to settle a dispute.

An appeals hearing is a detailed and informal review of Cliff Hanger's (or any taxpayer's) IRS audit. This review is to ensure that the examiner did not break any rules or overlook any procedures. The Appeals Officer looks only at balancing the merits of the issues the taxpayer raises in disagreement versus the merits of the case as presented by the IRS. If Mr. Hanger presents any new evidence to the Appeals Officer that the examiner in the audit did not see first, the Appeals Officer will simply transfer the case back to examination, where it will probably land on the desk of the examiner initially assigned to the audit.

During the appeals hearing process, the IRS Office of Appeals cannot engage in ex-parte communications. That is to say that the Appeals Officer cannot communicate about a taxpayer's case with any examinations officers, employees of the collections division, or any other division of the IRS without the Truly Troubled Taxpayer's knowledge. This serves to further enforce the fairness of the Appeals hearing and the impartiality of the Appeals Officer.

"Other than honestly, truthfully and thoroughly responding to the Appeals Officer's questions, how I can add to the appeals process?" Cliff wondered aloud, abruptly interrupting the Appeals Officer in mid-sentence. The Appeals Officer stopped talking and slowly raised his eyes from the documents on the table in front of him to meet Cliff's gaze "I'm sorry— did you hear that? I was just thinking aloud."

__Consider the Available Options__

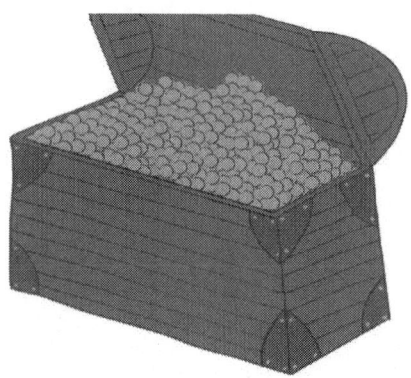

 *Some of the available alternatives to collections*

"Although the issues that you can bring up during your appeals hearing are limited," said the appeals officer in a gruff but well-intentioned tone of voice. Clearing his throat he continued, "You can challenge the proposed collections actions, or you could raise one of several other alternatives to the immediate collection of your hard-earned tax dollars by the IRS."

Cliff's mind began to drift. He imagined paying off his tax debt by finding a treasure chest filled with gold doubloons buried in his own backyard. Poof! *"Forget that,"* he thought, *"I'll never find that kind of money! Let's put our thinking cap on!"* He tried to think of a way to cash in on his largest asset – his house. "How about, like, taking out a home equity line of credit for home improvements to pay the IRS debt?"

The Appeals Officer's reply came swiftly: "Your primary residence is not an ATM you can use to pay the IRS. You probably will not be able to come up with all the money you owe the IRS all at once. Historically, this situation has been the case for more than one Truly Troubled Taxpayer. Congress, in their benevolence, codified several solutions into law, under Title 26"

"These alternatives exist so that a Truly Troubled Taxpayer, such as yourself, may be able to propose them to an Appeals Officer during the Collection Due Process hearing. Some of the more popular alternatives to collections are:

1. Offer In Compromise (the *"pennies on a dollar"* option)
2. Currently Not Collectable
3. Installment Agreements (including partial pay IAs)
4. Innocent Spouse treatment
5. Challenging the Underlying Tax Liability
6. Collections Appeal Program
7. Penalty Abatement or Abatement of Interest, and
8. Collection Due Process."

Cliff shook his head in amazement and asked, "Could you please repeat that for me?" The examiner did not miss a beat. "A more detailed discussion of each of these alternatives is covered in

Section II of *Defend Yourself with Confidence-How to Survive an IRS Audit*. Have you heard of the book?"

The mission of the Appeals Officer is to resolve the issues in a fair and impartial way that saves the IRS from the expense of having to go to US Tax Court. Prior to going to US Tax Court, a high percentage of all appeals hearings reach a settlement (90+% in my experience). One of the ways that settlement is possible in the appeals process is something called the 'hazards of litigation.' Going to US Tax Court is expensive. The appeals officer will carefully review the facts of every Truly Troubled Taxpayer's case and try to measure how much proof it would take a US Tax Court Judge to decide against the IRS. To go to US Tax Court, most taxpayers really need the assistance of a tax professional that is familiar with applying the Federal Rules of Evidence, such as a <u>United States Tax Court Practitioner</u> or a licensed tax attorney.

Alternatives to IRS Collections

 *Some of the available alternatives to collections*

Prior to going into a discussion of processing any issues with the IRS (your tax controversy case) through the court system, it is important to consider the many alternatives to the outright collection of tax dollars that are available to most taxpayers. I will discuss their various attributes and clarify that, with rare exception;

 There are no 'one-size-fits-all' solutions to tax problems.

Despite what your personal consumption of information on the mass media platform of your choice (radio, television, internet, etc.) may lead you to believe, pennies on the dollar does not make sense for everyone. Unless your legal name is *Penny Zahn Duh-DAH-lah*.

Offer in Compromise

Offer In Compromise, also known as the pennies on the dollar solution, works for *some* Truly Troubled Taxpayers. My experience is that not owning a house and not owning a car and not owning a cell phone in your personal name can lend some assistance in qualifying for an Offer in Compromise. Other situations are completely the opposite: the Truly Troubled Taxpayer who owns a brand new home on a construction loan, a mobile vacation home in sunny Florida, and practices as a certified minister who lives solely on the money collected in the Sunday church plate collection might also apply. It comes down to how your financials look to the IRS collections division that is in charge of reviewing your submission for an Offer in Compromise. There are a few primary types, described in the pages that follow.

OICDATC – Offer in Compromise Doubt as to Collectability – The fact that you really cannot pay your taxes in full is doubtful to the IRS – unless you know how to prove it to them! Doubt as to your ability to pay in full within the collection period allowed by law is used as a basis for the acceptance of this type of offer in compromise.

OICDCSC – Offer in Compromise Doubt as to Collectability with Special Circumstance – The basis for the acceptance of an offer like this is similar to the OICDATC discussed above, but special circumstances exist that warrants accepting the offer for less than the reasonable collection potential (RCP).

OICDATL – Offer in Compromise Doubt as to Liability – To the IRS, sincere doubt rarely exists whether or not the tax truly exists. Similarly, the IRS does not doubt that the tax was calculated to be totally correct. The basis used for the acceptance of this type of an offer relies on the fact that your tax debt may be called into doubt and proven to be entirely incorrect.

OICETA – Offer in Compromise Effective Tax Administration – The liability is correct and the tax debt can be paid in full. For the IRS to consider this option, requiring you to fully pay the tax would really have to either create an economic hardship for you or be an ugly public policy issue for the IRS. That equates to an individual who may be disabled, have a serious medical condition, or perhaps someone who is frail and elderly.

The Appeals Officer pushed a button on the remote control and what appeared to be a red inflatable Chinese dragon began to fill with air behind him. As it inflated, the shape wasn't like a Chinese dragon at all but began to form the shape of a curious question mark, with a sly smirk.

Currently Not Collectible

"This alternative is only available if your financial ability is limited to meeting your basic living expenses. If you can demonstrate an inability to pay your tax debt, your account may be marked currently not collectible, or CNC for short. Although your tax debt continues to remain a liability to be paid, the IRS refrains from enforcing any collections activities." Cliff Hanger began to catch on, quickly adding, "But all the penalties and interest continue to accrue for the remainder of time remaining in the period of time the IRS has by law to collect, right?" "True, true. Your tax debt may return to active collection status at any time. However, if you remain in CNC status until your statute expires (which could be up to 10 years), your tax debt vanishes. Disappears. Ceases to exist."

Cliff scratched his head and retorted, "But nobody wants to be *that* poor for *that* long a time," crossing his arms and letting out a subtle "humph!"

Then, in a smooth and quick flurry of motion, the Appeals Officer simultaneously snatched up the remote and kicked his feet up on top of the desk. "You should be aware," he remarked to Cliff, still transfixed by the inflatable question mark, "now we're going to go a little deeper into the weeds."

Challenge the Underlying Liability

"This is where most Truly Troubled Taxpayers begin to yawn and fall asleep on me," said the Appeals Officer. Cliff, hoping to find an alternative to collections that fit his particular tax situation, put his hands on the sides of the seat of the chair and sat up straight.

"If the tax return you filed with the IRS reported a tax due that remains unpaid, you can call this amount into dispute at a Collections Due Process (CDP) hearing with an appeals officer. Another example of how you can challenge the underlying tax liability is by filing a petition with the U.S. Tax Court in response to a Notice of Deficiency (NOD) that you received. You can also challenge the underlying tax liability when filing an OICDATL (which was addressed in this book on page 97), thus challenging whether or not you are responsible for paying for the underlying tax assessed by the IRS. Sound fair enough?" Cliff felt dazed, but felt his head begin to gently nod in agreement.

Payment Programs

The Appeals Officer reached into his right-hand desk drawer and pulled out a green visor and placed it atop his bean. "If you find yourself financially strapped or unable to pay – and I mean unable to pay **immediately** – all of the taxes you owe to the IRS, you may still have hope." The sound of the word hope was enough to wake Cliff from his slumber. "Wait a minute! Is it possible for me to set up an installment agreement and to make monthly installment payments to the IRS?"

"Well," the Appeals Officer continued, "as long as you are able to pay your tax debt in full over a 6-year period of time –that's 72 months if you're doing the math in your head -- setting up an installment agreement may be possible. Several types of installment agreements can be arranged with the IRS. However, before applying for any type of specific payment agreement, all of your tax returns must have been filed with the IRS, and you must be current. That is to say, you must have filed all of your past due or unfiled tax returns prior to setting up an installment agreement."

Streamlined Installment Agreements - SIA

Qualifying for a <u>streamlined installment agreement</u> is a much quicker and simplified method compared to all of the other types of installment agreements. It does not require that the IRS verify all of your financial assets, expenses, and income.

 Verification of your finances can usually be taken care of through the lengthy process of completing and submitting your financial information via <u>Form 433</u> or a <u>Collection Information Statement</u>.

For an SIA, it can be as easy as calculating the amount of one monthly payment. Begin by dividing the amount of the outstanding tax debt (plus penalties, plus interest) by 72. If a larger payment is affordable over a shorter period of time, the process is streamlined even more. The most important reason to pay off a balance due to the IRS in the shortest period of time possible all comes down to interest. The faster a tax debt is paid off, the less interest will be pais over the long run and the smaller amount of cash it will cost overall.

Pretend the amount of outstanding income tax debt, penalties, and interest owed to the IRS is $50,000 or less. This is the primary criteria the IRS uses to determine who qualifies to apply for an SIA online. Businesses, however, must owe $25,000 or less in taxes to qualify for an online SIA application. The period for making payments to fully obliterate your tax debt cannot exceed 72 months or 6 years. Other minor technical criteria exist for you to qualify for an SIA, but that sums up the basics.

The IRS, true to form, always charges a little tiny fee for setting up an installment agreement, and the fees vary depending on the type of agreement you want to setup. You can find the fee schedule at the IRS website or apply for an online payment agreement at https://www.irs.gov/individuals/online-payment-agreement-application.

Other Installment Agreements

If you're ineligible to apply for setting up an online payment agreement, you may still qualify to pay in installments, but this is where obtaining the assistance of a tax professional can really come in handy. You will find it impossible to negotiate an installment agreement with the IRS without providing them with some very detailed financial information by yourself. You must submit a report of your current financial condition to the IRS. The IRS uses this information to determine two things. First, they determine if you are a candidate for an installment agreement. Second, they determine if and how you can satisfy your outstanding tax debt within the period of time allowed by law.

Completing this very important and necessary form properly with the assistance of a knowledgeable Enrolled Agent can help you take advantage of the many expenses that most taxpayers often overlook. The reason these expenses are commonly overlooked is that they aren't included in the instructions for how to fill this form out. They are buried deep in the Internal Revenue Code and Internal Revenue Manual.

Because completing this form is such a complicated endeavor for most **self-employed individuals**, professional assistance is usually required. That is because, in addition to the same information required of wage-earning taxpayers, self-employed individuals need to prepare a current statement of their profit and loss. This is so the IRS can calculate and determine your current amount of income from what frequently equates to irregular cash flows. Self-employed individuals also need to provide their business bank account statements and prove the current fair market value of all their business assets.

"Boy!" Cliff remarked, "the requirements that need to be met for and installment agreement don't sound very easy to satisfy."

"Exactly!" the appeals officer replied. "Precisely because for every figure you assert on the financial information collections document, you need to provide **evidence to substantiate** that particular item of income or expense. This includes assets that you can take a loan against, an asset that you could sell in order to settle your current tax debt with the IRS, or property held by someone else on your behalf, like an IRA, 401(k), or any other tax-qualified assets intended to be spent during your retirement. "In addition," the Appeals Officer continued, casually returning his feet to the floor and bringing the remote control into plain view again, "as I previously mentioned, taking advantage of all the deductions against your income that are available to you, as a taxpayer, could make all the difference between qualifying for an installment agreement – or not."

By the look on his face, Mr. Cliff Hanger was perplexed. "Do you mean that by properly taking advantage of professional assistance in collecting my financial information, I might also unknowingly qualify for a suspension of collections activity? Maybe even – um – that currently not collectible status that you mentioned before?" Now it was the Appeals Officer's chance to slowly and gently nod his head.

Partial-Pay Installment Agreements

Although it seems like the IRS expects all taxpayers to pay down any and all delinquent tax debt immediately fully, most people find this expectation very unrealistic. If you can prove to the IRS that you cannot financially afford to pay your tax bill under the terms of a normal installment agreement, you might qualify for a Partial-Pay Installment Agreement. This involves the IRS agreeing to let you pay less than the total amount you owe through an installment agreement, and is a much more difficult installment agreement to obtain from the IRS. Once you are able to prove that your reasonable collection potential (RCP, the technical acronym used by the IRS) is less than your outstanding tax bill, then a Partial-Pay Installment Agreement could be your best friend and a potential solution to your tax problems. Properly calculating your RCP is the most important aspect of obtaining an outcome to result in your favor.

Innocent Spouse Considerations

The Appeals Officer opened up a music box, and some delicate music began to play. "When you are married, and you file your tax return as married filing joint, you and your spouse combine both of your income, deductions, credits, and exemptions on the same tax return. In filing your tax return with married filing joint status, each of you is both mutually and exclusively responsible for the entire tax associated with that return. That means the IRS can go after either one of you or both of you together equally or unequally to ensure that your tax debt is fully paid." The appeals licked his index right finger and then wiped it dry on his right eyebrow, and then his left. With a quick, deep inhale, he continued. "Even if you (or your spouse) claim that you (or they)

did not know of your better half's (or your) unreported income (which could have come from gambling, self-employment or embezzlement), the "innocent" spouse (that's *you*, right?) is still separately responsible for the entirety of the tax liability."

"As a remedy to situations like this that we are in, I have a pair of toothpicks. If you thought we were going deep into the weeds before, let me assure you that it really doesn't get any more detailed than this. The toothpicks are for your eyes if you need to keep them open." Cliff furrowed his brow and started to say, "Well…yeah… I mean…you know…umm," abruptly curtailing himself with "Okay. Okay. Go on." The appeals officer politely pulled the corners of his lips to the side as if to smile, but it looked like a smirk. With a gentle sigh, he said in a plainspoken voice, "Congress has put into law the innocent spouse relief provisions under IRC § 6015. Three types of relief are available for an innocent spouse (a.k.a. the "requesting spouse") under the innocent spouse relief provisions of The Internal Revenue Code. Innocent spouse treatment is also another potential doorway into filing a petition to have your case heard by the U.S. Tax Court."

Innocent Spouse – IRC § 6015(b)

IRC § 6015(b) innocent spouse relief offers the requesting spouse relief from tax attributable to the other (non- requesting) spouse.

A number of criteria must be satisfied in order to qualify. First, the original return filed must have been filed with married filing joint status and signed by both spouses. At the time the original tax return was signed by the requesting spouse, it must have contained an understatement of income that is solely attributable to the non-requesting spouse. The requesting spouse must not have known about the other sources of income from the non-requesting spouse when signing the original return. Also, it must be shown that it would be unfair to hold the requesting spouse liable for the tax. The time frame for requesting this type of innocent spouse treatment is restricted to within two years after the IRS begins collections activity. The requesting and non-requesting spouses can still be married when innocent spouse relief is requested.

Separation of Liability IRC § 6015(c)

IRC § 6015(c) separation of liability relief offers the potential of limiting the requesting spouse's exposure to the outstanding tax bill. Put another way, under IRC § 6015(c) the requesting spouse can limit their responsibility for paying the joint tax debt to pay tax only on the income amounts allocable to that same requesting spouse. Again, a number of hoops to jump through in order to qualify. Just like under IRC § 6015(b), the original tax return must have been filed with married filing joint status and signed by both spouses. The requesting spouse must not have known about the understatement or underpayment allocable to the non-requesting spouse when signing the original return. Additionally, it would not be reasonable for the requesting spouse to have any knowledge of the other sources of income or underpayment allocable to the non-requesting spouse when signing the original return. Finally, the requesting spouse must not have lived in the same residence with the non-requesting spouse for at least the past 12 months. That could be because they were divorced, legally separated, or the non-requesting spouse is dead - the requesting spouse is widowed. The time frame for requesting this type of innocent spouse treatment is restricted to within two years after the IRS begins collections activity. Incidentally, the non-requesting spouse cannot transfer assets to the requesting spouse one year prior to being called into audit if the only reason is to avoid tax or get away from paying taxes. This transfer would disqualify the requesting spouse from filing under IRC IRC § 6015(c).

Equitable Relief IRC § 6015(f)

Under IRC § 6015(f), the tax return must have been filed with married filing joint status. Even if relief is not available under either IRC § 6015(b) innocent spouse relief or under IRC § 6015(c) separation of liability, innocent spouse relief may still be available to the requesting spouse. Under this provision in the code, it would not be reasonable to expect the requesting spouse to have had any knowledge of the understatement or underpayment attributable to the non-requesting spouse when signing the original return. No disqualified assets can transfer to the requesting spouse. When the original return was filed, no fraudulent intent or purpose must have existed. Additionally, the limitation for filing within the first two years after IRS begins collections activity does not apply when claiming innocent spouse under IRC § 6015(f) equitable relief.

The Appeals Officer glanced down at the conference table. Two toothpicks lay undisturbed beside Cliff's now slumbering head. After clearing his throat, he reached under his chair for a megaphone and loudly pronounced, "WANT TO FIND OUT HOW TO AVOID ANOTHER PENALTY?"

Penalty Abatement

Tax penalties can substantially increase the balance that you owe to the IRS. This is because the IRS doesn't need to take your individual situation and circumstances into consideration when assessing penalties. However, you may still be able to get the IRS to <u>abate penalties</u> that would otherwise be applicable to you under a number of circumstances, particularly if you can show how, in your situation, you had a <u>reasonable cause</u>.

Abatement of tax penalties is generally granted when you can show that you exercised ordinary care and **prudence** but were unable to comply with fulfilling your obligations by filing and paying your taxes on time. Any reason or rationale other than the factors listed below, which come out of the Internal Revenue Manual (IRM), would be much more difficult for the IRS to find a reasonable cause for abating penalties.

- Fire, (IRM 20.1.1.3.2.2.2)
- Casualty, (IRM 20.1.1.3.2.2.2)
- Natural disaster or other disturbances, (IRM 20.1.1.3.2.2.2)
- Inability to obtain records, (IRM 20.1.1.3.2.2.3)
- Death, (IRM 20.1.1.3.2.2.1)
- serious illness, (IRM 20.1.1.3.2.2.1)
- incapacitation or hospitalization, (IRM 20.1.1.3.2.2.1)

- unavoidable absence of the taxpayer or a member of the taxpayer's immediate family, (IRM 20.1.1.3.2.2.1)
- Any other reason which establishes that you used all <u>ordinary business care and prudence</u> to meet your Federal tax obligations but were nevertheless unable to file or fully pay. (IRM 20.1.1.3.2.2)

 The IRS takes only certain facts into consideration in order to determine whether or not to apply the Reasonable Cause basis for underpayment of your taxes.

The IRS uses an automated system to provide consistency in the analytical process through which decisions are made regarding penalties. However, the IRS may be interested in the facts and circumstances that prevented you from filing your return or paying your tax during the period of time that you did not file or pay your taxes timely. Once you're able to establish and prove how the facts and circumstances of your life affected your ability to file and pay your taxes, the IRS would question what actions you took subsequently in order to file or pay your taxes. In addition to innocent spouse treatment, abatement of penalties is another potential door to filing a petition and having your case heard by the U.S. Tax Court.

 However, not all penalties fall under the Tax Court <u>jurisdiction</u>.

For instance, the Tax Court does not have the ability to make a legal decision on whether or not you are liable for the penalty for failure to **file** your income taxes on time.

As Cliff got into his car ready to go home, he received a chilling telephone call. It was the county coroner from two states away. Evidently, his sister and her boyfriend had passed away last evening in an automobile accident involving a tree. Cliff was responsible for paying for both funerals – one where his sister lived and one where they grew up together – out of pocket before the insurance proceeds were made available. This made Cliff fall behind on his regular schedule of making payments to the IRS. But Cliff had done his homework! He knew that death of an immediate family member was covered as a reasonable cause. However, in Mr. Cliff Hanger's case, he didn't get caught up on paying the IRS soon enough, and his request for **penalty abatement** fell on deaf ears with the IRS. Timing is everything. If only he had listened to his friend, the Enrolled Agent, instead of renovating the doorways of his house. Thankfully, he hadn't exhausted all his resources in finding a remedy to settling his tax debt.

The United States Tax Court

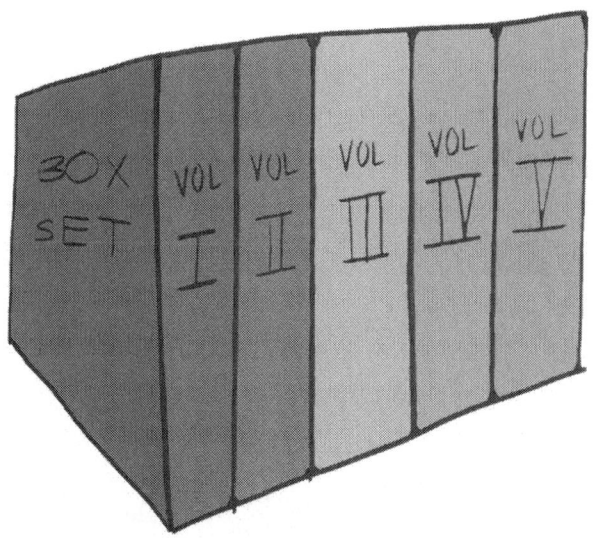

 *Often overlooked steps in preparing for US Tax Court*

This option comes last for a good reason. Your last stop in finding a remedy to your situation of tax controversy is the United States Tax Court ("USTC").

The U.S. Tax Court is a court of record established by Congress under the U.S. Constitution. When the IRS determines that you have a tax deficiency (you owe some money to the IRS), you might be able to dispute that deficiency in the Tax Court before paying any of the outstanding tax. However, your situation of tax controversy needs to fit through the doorway.

Four "doorways" can gain you access to having your case heard by the U.S Tax Court: a collection due process (CDP) hearing, a notice of deficiency (NOD), IRC § 6015 Innocent spouse considerations, and IRC § 6404 abatement of penalties. Whether or not you can file a petition with the United States Tax Court (USTC) relies on the timing of several factors. This is because each of these doorways has its own unique time constraints with which you must comply. You do not want to lose track of time only to find that your only window of opportunity has already closed. Once you are eligible to file a petition with the U.S. Tax Court, you will soon begin to realize that the Tax Court has its own set of Rules of Practice and Procedure.

The extent of the US Tax Court's ability to make legal decisions and judgments (Tax Court jurisdiction) is limited. The areas that Congress has specifically drafted legislation on to bestow general jurisdiction on the Tax Court include the areas of:

- When you owe any income taxes, estate taxes or gift taxes (IRC § 6213),
- Any additions to taxes that you might owe,
- Innocent spouse relief (covered earlier in this text),
- Abatement of interest (covered earlier in this text)

- Review of IRS liens and levies under Internal Revenue Code sections 6320 and 6330,
- To determine whether to treat an individual as an independent contractor or an employee,
- If the IRS has not refunded your overpayment of taxes after the tax court decided in your favor,
- Re-determining the amount of interest you owe the IRS,
- Modifying a decision regarding estate tax,
- Awards you are to receive for the costs of engaging the IRS in litigation,
- If the IRS tries to collect taxes on an issue you have already petitioned the Tax Court on,
- Very technical issues like transferor liability or fiduciary liability,
- Declaring whether or not your retirement plan qualifies as a retirement plan,
- Determining the tax-exempt status of an exempt organization,
- Whether an estate is eligible for paying an amount due for taxes in installment payments,
- The valuation of a gift for gift tax purposes,
- Large Partnership tax issues in TEFRA adjustment & re-adjustment cases,

- And so on, and so forth.

If you were issued a notice of deficiency (NOD) under Internal Revenue Code IRC § 6212 and you *timely* file a petition to the Clerk of the U.S. Tax Court, you might have a shot at having your case heard by the Tax Court. Keep in mind, however, that most (85-90%) of all tax court cases are settled in appeals before they even get to the courtroom.

So what happens next? If you have determined that the Tax Court has jurisdiction over your tax case, you must timely file a petition with the Tax Court, according to *Tax Court Rule 34*.

You will need to properly complete and submit a petition to the U.S. Tax Court. Filing a petition for a Tax Court case may seem like filling out any other piece of government paperwork. However, filling out the form and filing the petition is not as straightforward as it might seem.

The Tax Court Process

You commence a Tax Court case by "filing a petition with the Court." *Rule 20, Tax Court Rules* and the petition has to be filed on time for the Court to have jurisdiction of the case. But what's the time permitted by the court?

Let's say, for instance, that you receive a statutory notice of deficiency (NOD) because you did not respond to the 30-day letter following an audit. You now have 90-days from the IRS mailing date of the statutory notice of deficiency (NOD) to file a petition with the Tax Court.

What if instead, you received a Notice of Deficiency (NOD) after you had the opportunity for a collection due process hearing?

Under these circumstances, you must petition the USTC within 30 days of receiving your notice of deficiency (NOD). The time allowed to file a petition for each type of innocent spouse is different, and so is the time frame to timely file a petition for penalty abatement.

When you *timely file* your completed petition with the Tax Court, you need to make sure to include the current filing fee to the Clerk of the U.S. Tax Court and send it to their mailing address. Surprisingly, once your petition has been filed on time, sent to the proper address along with the correct filing fee, it may be asserted by the IRS or determined by the Tax Court, for a variety of different reasons, that the U.S. Tax Court simply does not have jurisdiction over your case.

The IRS has the right to challenge certain aspects of your petition. Counsel for the IRS is required to answer your petition within 60 days, according to Tax Court Rule 36. If you are required to respond to the IRS because they questioned certain aspects of your petition, you have 45 days to submit a reply (*Tax Court Rule 37*). After a 30-day breather of neither party exchanging any correspondence, formal discovery commences and can go on for months. Formal discovery must end 45 days (or 75 days, depending) before calendar call. Any formal motions must end 14 days before calendar call. Calendar call is the time when your case will be placed upon the court calendar for the judge to hear your side of the story. After calendar call concludes, a date will be scheduled for your case to be heard by the US Tax Court.

Cliff Hanger jumped through all the various hoops necessary to qualify his tax case to be heard by the U.S. Tax Court. On the bright side, after he filed a petition with the Tax Court within the time permitted by law, the IRS was not able to collect any money until the decision of the Tax Court was final.

Cliff found that the U.S. Tax Court Justice seemed to have more patience in explaining his situation than his situation or circumstances might have even deserved. However, by self-representing himself, Cliff took all the risks upon himself.

As is common in a many Small Tax Court cases, a swift judgment came from the bench against Mr. Hanger. That meant a court ordered demand for payment of all the tax, penalties and interest (the interest that has been accumulating throughout this lengthy process).The Tax Court process has caused even some of the wealthiest of Americans to go bankrupt.

Going to US Tax Court involves technical issues far too numerous to delve into for the purposes of this book. As is always the case, everyone's tax situation is unique and different.

This book has very briefly reviewed major steps involved in the process of an IRS audit, what goes on in an appeals hearing, most of the alternatives available to the collection of taxes, and a few of the technical aspects involved in getting your tax case heard by the U.S. Tax Court.

To help you resolve your tax problems and bring them to finality, seek out an Enrolled Agent, or United States Tax Court Practitioner. If you want to determine if your case might be eligible to be heard by the U.S. Tax Court, you should engage in the professional services of a United States Tax Court Practitioner or a tax attorney.

Thank you for reading this book. Please share your thoughts on social media.

Appendix A - What Are Your Rights?

The **Taxpayer Bill of Rights (TBOR)** was written in 1988 and was revised in 1996/1998 before it came out in its current form in 2014. The revisions are largely reflective of the number and type of complaints registered with Congress against the activities of the IRS. The TBOR is a set of 10 basic rights you should be aware of to have a better understanding of your rights in dealing with the IRS. This same list of your rights for the IRS processes of the audit, appeal, collection, and refunds can also be found in Publication 1. The IRS is supposed to send this out with any initial correspondence regarding your audit. In 2015, Congress added these taxpayer rights to the Internal Revenue Code.

1. **The Right to Be Informed** – of the amount you owe, split into tax, penalties and interest, and explained in technical language of law, as per IRC § 7521(b)(1), IRC § 7522, IRC § 6751(a) , IRC § 6402(I), IRC §§ 6212 & 6213(b).

2. **The Right to Quality Service** – You have the right to receive prompt, courteous, and professional assistance in your dealings with the IRS. That means you should be able to easily understand what's going on through clear and easily understandable communications from the IRS. If you feel like

you've received inadequate service from the examiner, you should file a complaint. The IRS has a mission statement: to provide America's taxpayers top quality service by helping them understand and meet their tax responsibilities and enforce the law with integrity and fairness to all.

The standard types of complaints can range from violating a law or rule of conduct to a more subjective complaint such as you feel you were treated discriminatorily by the IRS. If you feel that the IRS was in any way rude, over- zealous, excessively aggressive or if you felt they intimidated you, then you should get in line at the Taxpayer Advocate Service and make sure you're prepared to spill the beans.

3. **The Right to Pay No More than the Correct Amount of Tax** – If you feel you overpaid your taxes and you timely file a refund claim, you can ask for your money back. This must be done within a 3-year time period from the date you filed your return or 2 years from the date you paid the tax, whichever is later. This is otherwise known as the statute of limitations under IRC § 6511.

4.   **The Right to Challenge the IRS's Position and Be Heard** — This was covered in more detail earlier on in this book. You can present to the IRS the documents you used to arrive at the figures that appear on the tax return. The IRS is required to fairly take this into consideration, but they may still not agree with you. The IRS will then issue a statutory notice of deficiency (NOD) explaining what is causing your tax to increase. This NOD opens for you one of the four doorways for you to petition the U.S. Tax Court prior to paying the tax. (IRC § 6212). The petition needs to be filed within 90 days of the mailing date of the NOD.

Before the IRS begins collections activity on your tax debt by levying your bank account, the IRS must provide you with an opportunity for a hearing before an independent IRS Appeals officer. If you disagree with Appeals' determination, you can file a petition with the clerks of the US Tax Court. (IRC §§ 6320, 6330)

5.   **The Right to Appeal an IRS Decision in an Independent Forum** – You are entitled to a fair and impartial appeal at the administrative level for most IRS decisions against you. Regardless of what conclusions are drawn from your hearing, the appeals officer is required to notify you of the Office of Appeals decision in writing. You will generally be given a chance to file a

petition to US Tax Court within 90 days of the date this notice was sent out to you under IRC § 6213.

For the first four months after you file a petition to the tax court and as long as the appeals office did not issue you an NOD, the Office of Appeals has the ability to settle your case.

If you have paid your taxes in full and your claim to a tax refund is denied -- or if no action is taken on you claim within six months -- you may be able to file a refund suit in a United States District Court or the United States Court of Federal Claims. (IRC § 7422)

6. **The Right to Finality** – If the IRS can show that you filed a false or fraudulent tax return, there is no right to finality. They have until the end of time to assess tax. The IRS also has 10 years to collect on your tax debt. Yes, this is technically finality, but it takes virtually a lifetime for you to see the light of day on the other side of the tunnel. Generally, though, you have a right to know that the IRS has a maximum of three years from the date you filed a return to audit your return. You, similarly, have a three year period of time to file a claim for a refund (or two years after the tax was paid, whichever is later).

7. **The Right to Privacy** – Generally, you have a right that an examination is more intrusive and absolutely necessary. Unless the IRS can show that they can have a reasonable basis to believe that you have unreported income, the IRS should not probe for extraneous information about your lifestyle during an audit (IRC § 7602(e)). If the IRS wants to contact a third party, your boss for example, the examiner needs to provide you with a reasonable notice in advance of contacting your boss.

You are protected from the IRS seizing an amount of your wages that is equivalent to the standard deduction for your filing status plus any personal exemptions you took on your return.

The IRS cannot take your personal residence without first getting court approval. Also protected are your personal items, such as necessary schoolbooks, tools of your trade of business, clothing, undelivered mail and a certain amount of furniture and household items. The car that you use to transport yourself to work, church, the grocery store, and school is also protected from being taken from you(IRC § 6343(a)).

During A Collection Due Process hearing, the appeals officer is required to consider balancing the IRS's proposed collection actions with your concern that the IRS's collection actions are no more intrusive than necessary (IRC §§ 6320, 6330).

8.   **The Right to Confidentiality -** Unless you give them your permission, the IRS may not disclose your tax information to anybody else (IRC § 6103).

Additionally, unless the IRS gives you reasonable advance notice, they cannot talk to your employer, neighbors, or bank to obtain information about your tax liability (IRC § 7602(c)).

If your tax return preparer knowingly uses your tax information for any reason other than for tax preparation, they may be subject to criminal fines or go to jail (IRC § 7216).

9.   **The Right to Retain Representation** – If you engage the services of an Enrolled Agent, attorney, or CPA to represent you in an audit with the IRS, you do not need to attend a face-to-face interview with your representative.

10.   **The Right to a Fair and Just Tax System** - If you cannot pay your tax debt in full and you meet certain conditions, you can

enter into a payment plan with the IRS. This is where you pay a set amount on a monthly basis over a period of time (IRC § 6159).

To find out more about the TBOR and what it means to you, visit: http://www.taxpayeradvocate.irs.gov.

Appendix B - Audit Letters

It should be noted that the IRS is prone to change the numbers, names, and descriptions of notices such as these with the frequency and consistency of someone who absentmindedly doodles different patterns on a piece of paper while talking on the telephone. Duly noted, this list in this appendix is a far cry from a complete list of letters or notices one could receive from the IRS.

Notice CP75A
The IRS is auditing your tax return and needs documentation to verify the Earned Income Credit (EIC), dependent exemption(s) and filing status you claimed.

Notice CP87A
The IRS received a tax return from another taxpayer claiming a dependent or qualifying child with the same social security number as a dependent or qualifying child listed on your tax return. The last four digits of the social security number for each dependent or qualifying child we're concerned about is shown on the notice for your review.

Letter 566
The IRS needs more information to process your application for an Individual Taxpayer Identification Number (ITIN). You may

have sent them an incomplete form, or you may have sent them the wrong documents, or you may not have signed the form.

Letter 2202
The IRS uses Letter 2202 to inform you of a field audit.

Letters 2205-A & 3572
The IRS uses Letters 2205-A & 3572 to inform you of a field audit & gives you the agent's name, phone, fax & office address.

Form 886A
The purpose of Form 886A is to request information from you during an audit or explain proposed adjustments in an audit.

Form 4564
The IRS uses Form 4564 to request information from you in an audit. The Form is called an Information Document Request (IDR)

Form 4549 & 5278
The IRS uses both Form 4549 & Form 5278 when the IRS has determined the changes to return at the close of an audit. Both are used to either propose changes to your return in an audit or as support for the issuance of a Notice of Deficiency.

Letter 3219 & Letter 531-T
If you don't agree with the results of the audit, the IRS will determine that you owe taxes and issue a Letter 3219 or Letter 531-T, known as a Notice of Deficiency.

Letter 1912
IRS Letter 1912 is just a cover letter for a Form 4549.

Letter 3254
This is sent for an initial face-to-face appointment for an IRS field exam.

Appendix C – Collections Letters

Please note: The IRS is prone to change the numbers, names, and descriptions of notices such as these with the frequency and consistency of someone who absentmindedly doodles different patterns on a piece of paper while talking on the telephone. Duly noted, this list in this appendix is a far cry from a complete list of letters or notices one could receive from the IRS.

Notice CP14
This notice informs you of a balance due.

Notice CP15
This notice informs you the IRS has asserted a penalty against you.

Notice CP39
This notice informs you the IRS has taken your spouse's or ex-spouse's refund to be applied to other taxes.

Notice CP42
This notice informs you the IRS has taken your refund to be applied to your spouse's or ex-spouse's other tax debt.

Notice CP44
This notice informs you the IRS is delaying your refund until they determine whether you owe other taxes.

Notice CP49
This notice informs you that the IRS has taken your refund to be applied to other taxes.

Notice CP71A-D
This notice reminds you of taxes owed.

Notice CP90
A Notice of Intent to Levy to warn you the IRS intends to take your assets and property.

Notice CP91
A Notice of Intent to Levy to warn you the IRS intends to take your Social Security check.

Notice CP92
This notice notifies you that the IRS has taken your refund to pay for other taxes and the notice invites you to appeal this seizure (via Collection Due Process)

Notice CP297
This notice notifies you that the IRS intends to levy your assets for unpaid taxes. You have the right to request a Collection Due Process (CDP) hearing.

Notice CP297-A
This notice notifies you that the IRS already levied your assets for unpaid taxes. You have the right to request a Collection Due Process (CDP) hearing.

Notice CP298
This notice notifies you that the IRS intends to levy up to 15% of your Social Security benefits for unpaid taxes.

Notice CP501
This notice reminds you of past due taxes.

Notice CP503
This notice informs you for the 2nd time that the IRS expects payment of past due taxes.

Notice CP504
This notice is an URGENT notice to inform you that the IRS intends to levy against your assets.

Notice CP521
This notice reminds you of payment.

Notice CP523
This notice informs you that your installment agreement has defaulted and the IRS intends to levy against your assets.

CP2000

You receive this letter when the IRS information on file doesn't match the information you reported on your tax return. This could cause an increase or decrease in your tax, or may not change it at all. You need to file your protest within 30 days from the date of this letter in order to appeal the proposed adjustments with the Office of Appeals.

Letter 484C

This letter informs you that the IRS denied you an installment agreement for your proposed amount but proposes a higher offer amount for you to agree to pay.

Letter 1058

This letter is the IRS's final notice that it intends to seize your property & money.

Letter 1741

This letter is to delay a payment agreement for you & to request that you call the IRS to discuss your income and expense information.

Letter 2050

This letter asks you to call the IRS about your overdue taxes or past due taxes.

Letter 2272C
This letter informs you that the IRS denied your installment agreement.

Letter 2273C
This letter explains some aspect of an installment agreement.

Letter 3172
This letter informs you the IRS has filed a federal tax lien.

Letter 3174
This letter is a reminder of taxes due after the IRS has already sent a Notice of Intent to Levy.

Letter 3228
This letter is a reminder of past due taxes.

Form 668(Y)(c)
This letter gives notice to the world that a tax lien exists against your property.

Form 668(W)(c)
This letter notifies your employer and you of a levy against your wages.

Form 668-A(c)
This letter notifies your bank and you of a bank levy with Form 668-A(c).

Form 8519
This letter notifies your bank and you of a bank levy.

Notice LT11
This letter is the IRS's final notice that it intends to seize your property & money.

Notice LT14
This letter reminds you of past due taxes and to request that you call the IRS.

Notice LT16
This letter informs you that the IRS has assigned your case to enforced collection action.

Appendix D – Letters/Notices with Appeals Rights

Please note: It should be noted that the IRS is prone to change the numbers, names, and descriptions of notices such as these with the frequency and consistency of someone who absentmindedly doodles different patterns on a piece of paper while talking on the telephone. Duly noted, this list in this appendix is a far cry from a complete list of letters or notices one could receive from the IRS.

Letter 11 – Final Notice of Intent to Levy and Notice of Your Right to a Hearing

This letter is to notify you of your unpaid taxes and that the IRS intends to levy to collect the amount owed. In order to appeal the proposed action with the Office of Appeals, you need to file a Form 12153, Request for A Collection Due Process Hearing, and send it to the address shown on your levy notice within 30 days from the date of the letter.

Letter 525 – General 30 Day Letter

This letter is accompanied by a computation report of proposed adjustments to your tax return. It outlines your options if you do not agree with the proposed adjustments. In order to appeal the proposed adjustments with the Office of Appeals, you need to file your protest within 30 days from the date of this letter.

Letter 531 – Notice of Deficiency

You will get this letter if you owe additional tax or other amounts for the tax year(s) listed in the letter. If you want to dispute the adjustments without payment, you will have 90 days from the notice date to file a petition with the Tax Court.

Letter 692 – Request for Consideration of Add'l Findings
You will get this letter with a computation report of proposed adjustments to your tax return. It outlines your options if you do not agree with the proposed adjustments. If you do not agree and in order to appeal the proposed adjustments with the Office of Appeals, you need to file your protest within 15 days from the date of this letter.

Letter 915 – Letter to Transmit Examination Report
This letter explains adjustments in the amount of tax. In order to appeal the proposed adjustments with the Office of Appeals, you need to file your protest within 30 days from the date of this letter.

Letter 950 – 30 Day Letter-Straight Deficiency or Over-Assessment

This letter is used for un-agreed, straight deficiency, straight over-assessment or mixed deficiency and over-assessment cases. You need to file your protest within 30 days from the date of this letter in order to appeal the proposed adjustments with the Office of Appeals.

Letter 1058 – Final Notice Reply within 30 Days

This letter is to notify you of your unpaid taxes and that the Service intends to levy to collect the amount owed. You need to file a Form 12153, Request for A Collection Due Process Hearing and send it to the address shown on your levy notice within 30 days from the date of the letter in order to appeal the action with the Office of Appeals.

Letter 1085 – 30-Day Letter Proposed 6020(b) Assessment

This letter is to notify you of your unpaid taxes and that the Service intends to levy to collect the amount owed. You need to file a Form 12153, Request for A Collection Due Process Hearing and send it to the address shown on your levy notice within 30 days from the date of the letter in order to appeal the action with the Office of Appeals.

Letter 1153 – Trust Funds Recovery Penalty Letter

This letter explains that the IRS's efforts to collect the federal employment or excise taxes due from the business named on the letter have not resulted in full payment of the liability. You need to file your protest within 60 days from the date of the letter in order to appeal this decision with the Office of Appeals.

Letter 3016 – IRC § 6015 Preliminary Determination Letter
This letter is a preliminary letter giving you 30 days to appeal the determination for innocent spouse relief under IRC § 6015. You need to file your protest within 30 days from the date of this letter in order to appeal the proposed adjustments with the Office of Appeals.

Letter 3391 – 30-Day Non-filer Letter
This letter advises you the IRS believes you are liable for filing tax returns for the periods identified in the letter. You need to file your protest within 30 days from the date of this letter in order to appeal the proposed adjustments with the Office of Appeals.

Letter 3172 – Notice of Federal Tax Lien Filing and Your Rights to a Hearing under IRC 6320
This letter is to notify you the IRS filed a notice of tax lien for the unpaid taxes. You need to file a Form 12153, Request for A Collection Due Process Hearing and send it to the address shown on your lien notice within 30 days from the date of the letter in order to appeal the action with the Office of Appeals.

NOTICES
CP 90 – Final Notice of Intent to Levy
CP 90 notifies you of your unpaid taxes and that the IRS intends to levy to collect the amount owed. You need to file a Form 12153, Request for A Collection Due Process Hearing and send it to the address shown on your levy notice within 30 days from the date of the letter in order to appeal the action with the Office of Appeals.

CP 92 – Notice of Levy upon Your State Tax Refund
CP 92 notifies you that the IRS levied your state tax refund to pay your unpaid federal taxes. You need to file a Form 12153, Request for A Collection Due Process Hearing and send it to the address shown on your levy notice within 30 days from the date of the letter in order to appeal the action with the Office of Appeals.

CP 242 – Notice of Levy upon Your State Tax Refund
CP 242 notifies you that the IRS levied your state tax refund to pay your unpaid federal tax. You need to file a Form 12153, Request for A Collection Due Process Hearing and send it to the address shown on your levy notice within 30 days from the date of the letter in order to appeal the action with the Office of Appeals.

CP 523 – IMF Installment Agreement Default Notice

CP 523 notifies you that the IRS intends to terminate your installment agreement in 30 days. You have the right to request an appeal if you do not agree by following the instructions in the notice.

Glossary

30 Day Letter
A letter that contains instructions on how to appeal the amount the IRS says you owe them. This letter may also be received if you ignore an IRS audit.

90 Day Letter
A letter from the Internal Revenue Service that advises you about an underpayment in an income tax or estate and gift tax debt for which you are responsible to pay, plus any penalties and interest.

Abate Penalties
To remove penalties owed.

Appeals
The Office of Appeals is an independent organization within the IRS whose mission is to help resolve tax disagreements between taxpayers and the Government. Every year, the Office of Appeals helps more than 100,000 taxpayers resolve their tax disputes without going to Tax Court.

Audit
A review or examination of the mathematical correctness of your tax return to ensure information is reported correctly according to the tax laws and to verify the reported amount of tax is correct.

Audit Notification Letter
Should your account be selected for audit, the IRS will notify you by mail. They don't initiate an audit by telephone.

Audit Technique Guide
Audit Techniques Guides (ATGs) help IRS examiners during audits by providing insight into issues and accounting methods unique to specific industries. While ATGs are designed to provide guidance for IRS employees, they're also useful to small business owners and tax professionals who prepare returns.

Auditor
Tax auditors evaluate your financial records to ensure that they are in compliance with applicable tax laws.

Calendar Call
A courtroom procedure in which the judge or a court officer calls out the names of the cases on the calendar is advised by the parties or their lawyers whether they are ready to proceed, and, if they are, sets a date for trial.

Certified Return Receipt
USPS certified receipt that provides evidence of delivery (to whom it was delivered and the date of delivery) and is available at the time of mailing with Certified Return Receipt.

Clerk Of The US Tax Court
The Office of the Clerk of the Tax Court answers all non-technical questions, including procedural, case-related, or general questions about the Court.

Collection Due Process Hearing
A Collection Due Process Hearing, also known as a CDP hearing, may be your last best chance to resolve a dispute you have with the IRS short of going to US Tax Court. Generally, the IRS must issue a Notice of Intent to Levy and Right to Request a Hearing if it sends a levy.

Collection Information Statement
A tool used by the IRS to determine how much you earn, how much you spend, what you own and who you owe.

Collections
If you don't pay your tax in full when you file your tax return, you'll receive a bill for the amount you owe. This bill starts the collection process, which continues until your account is paid in full or until the IRS may no longer legally collect the tax; for example, when the period of time for IRS collection expires.

Courtesy Disconnect
A courtesy disconnect is when the IRS switchboard gets overloaded, and the system hangs up on callers, as a matter of courtesy.

CPA
Certified Public Accountant (CPA) is a designation given by the American Institute of Certified Public Accountants to those who have passed an exam and met work experience requirements.

Currently Not Collectible
When you agree with the IRS that you owe taxes, but you are able to prove that your current financial situation doesn't allow you to pay what is due. While your account is in CNC status, the IRS will generally not engage in collection activity.

Department Of The Treasury
The Department of the Treasury is an executive department of the United States federal government. It was established by an Act of Congress in 1789 to manage government revenue.

Enrolled Agent
An enrolled agent is a person who has earned the privilege of representing taxpayers before the Internal Revenue Service by passing a three-part comprehensive IRS test covering individual and business tax returns, ethics and representation before the IRS.

Evidence To Substantiate
The responsibility to prove entries, deductions, and statements made on your tax returns are known as the burden of proof. You must be able to prove (substantiate) certain elements of expenses to deduct them. Your burden of proof is satisfied by having the information and receipts (where

needed) for the expenses claimed. You should keep adequate records to prove your expenses or have sufficient evidence that will support your own statement. You generally must have documentary evidence, such as receipts, canceled checks, or bills, to support your expenses

Examiner
Tax examiners and collectors, and revenue agents ensure that federal, state, and local governments get their tax money from businesses and citizens. They review tax returns, conduct audits, identify taxes owed, and collect overdue tax payments.

Face-To-Face Audit
A face-to-face audit is an in-person interview to review your records. The interview may be at an IRS office (office audit) or at your home, place of business, or accountant's office (field audit).

Field Audit
A field audit is a systematic investigation by the IRS that is conducted at your place of business or at the office of the individual who prepared your return.

Form 433-F
A tool used by the IRS to determine how much you earn, how much you spend, what you own and who you owe.

Form 4549
Form 4549 is a basic report form that is issued as a part of the examiner's first income tax report. Its key role is to report the examiner's findings in your audit and to propose adjustments to your income tax return. Also a form that can be used to agree to the changes on income tax return.

Formal Discovery
The Tax Court's Rules provide for formal pretrial discovery through the use of written interrogatories, requests for production of documents or things, and depositions in certain circumstances. The discovery process in Tax Court is less formal than in other courts of law.

Hell
Greek term widely used to denote the deity of the underworld and the abode of the dead.

IRS Office Of Appeals
An independent organization within the IRS whose mission is to help taxpayers and the US Government (IRS) resolve tax disagreements.

Income Tax Audits
An IRS audit is a review/examination of an organization's or individual's accounts and financial information to ensure information is represented correctly and the correct amount of tax is paid.

Income Tax Return
A document you file with the Internal Revenue Service or your state tax board reporting your income, profits, and losses of your business and other deductions, as well as details about your tax refund or tax liability. A 1040 form is an example of a federal income tax return commonly filed by individual taxpayers.

Information Document Request (IDR)
IDR stands for Information Document Request. An IDR is issued on IRS Form 4564. The IRS uses this form during a tax audit to request information from you. In reading this form, many people commonly misunderstand and reason that they need to supply a lot more information than is entirely necessary, but everyone's tax situation is different. This may not be the case for you.

Innocent Spouse
A spouse that can prove that his or her behavior did not produce they are not responsible for the tax bill and did not somehow benefit from the failure to pay the tax bill.

Installment Agreement
When you're financially unable to pay your tax debt immediately, you can apply to make monthly payments through an installment agreement. Before applying for any of the many payment agreements available, you must file have currently filed all your required tax returns.

Interest

If the IRS finds that you owe any tax, penalty, or interest, while processing your income tax return, you will receive a bill. Generally, interest accrues on any unpaid tax from the due date of the return until the date of payment is made in full. The interest rate is determined quarterly and is the federal short-term rate plus 3%. Interest compounds DAILY.

Internal Revenue Code

The Internal Revenue Code (IRC), formally the Internal Revenue Code of 1986, is the domestic portion of federal statutory tax law in the United States, published in various volumes of the United States Statutes at Large, and separately as Title 26 of the United States Code (USC).

Internal Revenue Manual

The Internal Revenue Manual (IRM) is considered by many to be the IRS bible. An official book of very detailed internal guidelines for people employed by the United States Internal Revenue Service (IRS).

IRS

Established in 1862 by President Abraham Lincoln, the agency operates under the authority of the United States Department of the Treasury, and its primary purpose includes the collection of individual income taxes and employment taxes.

IRS Audit
An IRS audit is a review/examination of an organization's or individual's accounts and financial information to ensure information is reported correctly according to the tax laws and to verify the reported amount of tax is correct.

IRS Examiner
Reviews tax returns for correctness and completeness, reviews and codes tax returns for computer processing, resolves errors and corresponds with taxpayers to obtain any missing information.

IRS Revenue Agent
Usually, an IRS Revenue Agent is an accountant who works for the U.S. Internal Revenue Service (IRS). A revenue agent's job is to examine and audit the financial records of individuals, businesses, and corporations to make sure that tax liabilities have been met.

Jurisdiction
Jurisdiction empowers the recipient with the official power to make legal decisions and judgments.

Line By Line Audit
An audit in which the IRS goes over every detail of every line on your income tax return

Market Segment Specialization Program
An IRS method used to focus on developing highly trained examiners for a particular market segment. A market segment may be an industry such as construction or entertainment, a profession like attorneys or real estate agents or an issue like passive activity losses.

Married Filing Joint Status
Married couples can combine and report both of their incomes, exemptions, and deductions on the same tax return.

National Research Project Audit
An audit conducted by the Internal Revenue Service (IRS) where they look at every single line item of your return and make sure you are able to prove each item in detail. Probably something you don't want to wish upon even your worst enemy.

Notice of Deficiency (NOD)
A Notice of Deficiency (NOD) is sometimes also called a 90-day letter or "statutory notice of deficiency," because it gives you 90 days to dispute or challenge the tax assessment and is authorized in Internal Revenue Code section 6212. You have a statutory (that means it's the law) 90-day window from the date of the notice to either agree to the government's adjustments or file a petition with the Tax Court for a redetermination of your tax deficiency. If the letter is addressed to you when you are outside the United States, the period is automatically extended to 150 days. If you fail to agree to the adjustments or to timely file a petition with the

US Tax Court, this will result in the assessment of the unpaid taxes and IRS actions to pursue collection activity.

Offer In Compromise-Doubt As To Collectability

An offer in compromise (OIC) is an agreement between you and the Internal Revenue Service that settles your tax debt for less than the full amount owed. This particular IRS Settlement option may be available if your assets and income are less than the full amount of the tax debt assessed by the IRS.

Offer in Compromise - Doubt As To Collectability (With Special Circumstance)

An offer in compromise (OIC) is an agreement between you and the Internal Revenue Service that settles your tax debt for less than the full amount owed. This IRS Settlement option may be potentially available to you if you do not believe the back taxes you owe are correct, taking into account any special circumstance[s] due to your age and your state of health.

Offer in Compromise - Doubt As To Liability

An offer in compromise (OIC) is an agreement between you and the Internal Revenue Service that settles your tax debt for less than the full amount owed. This IRS Settlement option may apply if you do not believe the back taxes you owe are correct of if you have a legitimate doubt that you owe any part or all the tax debt.

Office Audit
An office audit is an examination of your records by the Internal Revenue Service to ensure your compliance with tax laws. In an office audit, the IRS interviews you and inspects your records at an IRS office, where the seating arrangements are made to be as comfortable as possible, taking into consideration their budget.

Ordinary And Necessary
Generally, business expenses that are ordinary and necessary expenses of carrying on a trade or business are tax deductible. Internal Revenue Code (IRC or the "Code") § 162 allows deductions for ordinary and necessary trade or business expenses paid or incurred during the course of a taxable year.

Ordinary Business Care And Prudence
Being a responsible person and having plans to reasonably provide for meeting your future business obligations, you promptly report your income and expenses as they occur (as long as the future course of events is within reason).

Penalties
The United States income tax system is a pay-as-you-go tax system, which means that you must pay income tax as you earn or receive your income during the year. If you don't pay your tax or you pay an insufficient amount of tax through withholding, you may face various penalties for failures related to meeting various tax matters based on the

amount of tax not properly paid. The Internal Revenue Service (IRS) is primarily responsible for charging these penalties at the Federal level.

Penalty Abatement
To remove penalties owed.

Petition
A formal written request, filed with the US Tax Court, in response to an IRS notice of deficiency or notice of determination.

Phishing
Phishing is a scam typically carried out through unsolicited email or websites that pose as legitimate sites and lure unsuspecting victims to provide personal and financial information. The IRS recommends you report all unsolicited email claiming to be from the IRS or an IRS-related function to phishing@irs.gov.

Prudence
An accounting concept that requires promptly reporting your income and expenses as they occur.

Publication 1
A document published by the Internal Revenue Service that identifies your rights as a taxpayer and outlines the processes followed by the IRS when it audits or examines your tax return, issues a refund or collects taxes, as well as the appeals process that you can initiate.

Random Audit
Although the IRS continues to use random selection and computer screening based on statistical data to select returns for audits, an overly popularized urban myth continues to circulates that the IRS could just pick your tax return out of thin air. They always have a reason. More than likely multiple reasons or "flags" for an audit on your return that point to a more realistic reason why your (or your neighbor's) return was selected for audit by the IRS.

Reasonable Cause
When deciding whether or not to abate a tax penalty because of reasonable cause, the IRS looks at several discrete circumstances. The circumstances that the IRS is most likely to accept are listed in the text of this book.

Reasonable Collection Potential
The technical term for the tool the IRS uses to measure your ability to pay is called your Reasonable Collection Potential. The RCP is a value that can include money that can be squeezed out of investments, real estate, automobiles, bank accounts, and other property. In addition, the RCP also includes your anticipated future income, less certain amounts allowed for basic living expenses such as a bar of soap, a toothbrush, bread, and water.

Revenue Agent
Typically a person who possesses an accounting degree or who is trained as an accountant who works for the U.S. Internal Revenue Service (IRS). A revenue agent's job is to examine and audit the financial records of individuals, businesses, and corporations to make sure that tax liabilities have been met.

Revenue Agent's Report
Revenue Agent Reports (RARs) should contain all the information necessary for you to have a clear understanding of the IRS adjustments made to your return and to demonstrate how the tax debt was computed.

Revenue Officer
The IRS Agent who makes house calls is called an IRS Revenue Officer (or an IRS Revenue Agent - they make house calls too!). This IRS Agent typically shows up at your home or place of business when you are in debt to the IRS for an amount of $25,000 or greater.

Root Canal
If you get audited, your best bet is to seek out a qualified tax professional. But if you're a do-it-yourself type of person, you should anticipate experiencing the sensation of having your nerves removed without Novocain while your tax return is being cleansed by the IRS examiner. Smile!

Self-Employed Individuals
A person who works for themselves instead of working for an employer that pays a salary or a wage. A self-employed individual earns income through conducting profitable operations from a trade or business that they operate directly.

Statutory Notice Of Deficiency
A notice of deficiency is sometimes also called a 90-day letter or "statutory notice of deficiency," because it gives you 90 days to dispute or challenge the tax assessment and is authorized in Internal Revenue Code section 6212. You have a statutory 90-day window from the date of the notice to either agree to the government's adjustments or to file a petition with the US Tax Court for a redetermination of your tax debt. If the letter is addressed to you when you are outside the United States, the period is automatically extended to 150 days. Failing to agree to the adjustments or timely file a petition will result in the IRS assessing the tax debt and beginning collection activity.

Streamlined Installment Agreement
The streamlined installment agreement is part of the IRS' "Fresh Start Program." You need to have filed all your tax returns, and you must agree to file your tax returns on time and pay your taxes on time in the future. The main benefit of a streamlined installment agreement is that the IRS does not require you to complete a financial collection information statement so they can analyze your current financial

situation. You may be eligible to apply for an online payment agreement if you (as an individual) owe less than $50,000 or less in combined individual income tax, penalties, and interest, as well as have filed all required returns. The threshold amount for businesses is half of that or $25,000 or less in payroll taxes, and the business entity must have filed all required returns. If you (or your business) meet these simple requirements, you may be able to apply for an installment payment agreement on the internet.

Tax Attorney
Tax lawyers help individuals and organizations resolve federal, state, local, and international tax issues. Typically, they operate when dealing with larger tax debts and larger retainers to engage in their services.

Tax Compliance Officer
Tax compliance officers are employees of the Internal Revenue Service (IRS) who determine if businesses and individuals have paid the proper amount of taxes. The IRS provides tax compliance officers with substantial training.

Tax Court
A specialized court of law that hears and issues judgments on tax-related disagreements and related issues. The tax court in the United States is a federal court established by Congress to provide a judicial forum where

you as an individual or entity can contest a tax debt determined by the Internal Revenue Service before paying the disputed amount.

Tax Court Jurisdiction
The US Tax Court has the official power to make legal decisions and judgments regarding your tax debt. These judgments may involve the valuation of real property, the amount of tax the IRS seeks to collect, or the tax status of a pension plan or a charitable organization. The Tax Court's jurisdiction is generally prescribed by Internal Revenue Code section 7442, but specific grants of jurisdiction to the US Tax Court are interspersed throughout the Internal Revenue Code (the Code).

Tax Law
The rules, policies, and laws that oversee the tax process, which involves taxes on estates, transactions, property, income, licenses and more by the US government.

Tax Penalties
The United States income tax system is a pay-as-you-go tax system, which means that you must pay income tax as you earn or receive your income during the year. If you don't pay your tax or you pay an insufficient amount of tax through withholding, you may face various penalties for failures related to meet various tax matters based on the amount of tax not properly paid. The Internal Revenue Service (IRS) is primarily responsible for charging these penalties at the Federal level.

Taxpayer Bill Of Rights
The Taxpayer Bill of Rights groups the existing rights in the tax code into ten fundamental rights, and makes them as clear and understandable as an incredibly vague and slightly faded bumper sticker.

The United States Tax Court Practitioner
A non-attorney admitted to practice before the US Tax Court.

Unlimited Practice Rights
Unlimited representation rights allow a credentialed tax practitioner to represent you before the IRS on any tax matter. This is true no matter who prepared your return. Credentialed tax professionals who have unlimited representation rights include Enrolled Agents (EAs), Certified Public Accountants (CPAs), and Attorneys.

USPS Mail
USPS stands for United States Postal Service regular mail.

USTCP
United States Tax Court Practitioner

Index

3

30 Day Letter, 146, 147, 153

A

alternatives to collections, vii, viii, 93

appeals, vii, viii, x, 29, 74, 75, 81, 82, 86, 87, 89, 90, 92, 94, 102, 107, 110, 111, 123, 127, 131, 134, 167

audit, vii, viii, xi, 5, 6, 11, 15, 16, 17, 19, 20, 21, 22, 23, 24, 25, 26, 27, 28, 29, 31, 32, 33, 34, 35, 37, 38, 39, 42, 46, 55, 59, 61, 62, 64, 66, 71, 72, 73, 74, 75, 77, 80, 81, 83, 86, 89, 113, 124, 127, 128, 132, 133, 135, 137, 138, 153, 154, 158, 159, 160, 162, 163, 165, 167, 168

audit notification letter, 33

Audit Technique Guide, 65, 154

auditor, 37, 62, 80

C

collection due process, 120, 125

collections, ix, x, 10, 30, 81, 83, 90, 92, 96, 100, 102, 107, 108, 112, 113, 114, 131

compliance, 154, 165, 171

currently not collectible, 100, 108

D

Department of the Treasury, 5, 6, 157, 161

E

Enrolled Agent, x, 10, 28, 29, 30, 73, 78, 106, 118, 127, 135, 157

examiner, 5, 7, 21, 23, 24, 28, 31, 32, 33, 35, 37, 38, 46, 48, 53, 54, 59, 60, 61, 68, 71, 72, 73, 74, 75, 76, 77, 78, 80, 81, 85, 86, 89, 93, 129, 133, 158, 169

F

face-to-face audit, 62, 77

field audit, 26, 27, 158

I

IDR, 33, 59, 62, 137, 160

income tax, vii, x, 3, 15, 19, 31, 38, 43, 61, 68, 74, 105, 153, 158, 160, 161, 163, 166, 171, 172

income tax audits, vii, x, 19

information document, 20

innocent spouse, 111, 113, 117, 125, 149

installment agreement, 104, 106, 107, 108, 109, 142, 143, 152, 160, 170

interest, 54, 55, 56, 67, 101, 105, 121, 122, 126, 128, 153, 161, 171

Internal Revenue Code, ix, 41, 44, 45, 80, 84, 107, 111, 121, 123, 128, 161, 164, 165, 170, 172

Internal Revenue Manual, ix, 24, 62, 107, 116, 161

IRC §, 41, 43, 44, 45, 46, 47, 48, 49, 86, 128, 131, 132, 133, 134, 135

IRS, iii, iv, vii, viii, ix, x, 3, 4, 5, 6, 7, 8, 9, 10, 11, 12, 13, 14, 15, 16, 17, 19, 20, 21, 22, 23, 26, 27, 28, 29, 30, 31, 32, 33, 34, 35, 37, 38, 39, 40, 42, 43, 46, 53, 59, 61, 62, 63, 64, 68, 71, 72, 73, 74, 75, 76, 77, 78, 79, 80, 81, 82, 83, 84, 85, 86, 89, 90, 92, 93, 94, 95, 96, 97, 98, 100, 102, 104, 105, 106, 107, 108, 110, 112, 113, 114, 116, 117, 118, 120, 121, 122, 124, 125, 126, 127, 128, 129, 130, 131, 132, 133, 134, 135, 136, 137, 138, 139, 140, 141, 142, 143, 144, 145, 146, 149, 150, 151, 153, 154, 155, 156, 157, 158, 159, 160, 161, 162, 163, 164, 165, 166, 167, 168, 169, 170, 171, 172, 173

IRS audit, ix ,62, 71, 75

IRS examiner, 61, 72, 85

J

jurisdiction, 117, 121, 123, 124, 125, 172

N

NOD, 75, 81, 83, 85, 102, 121, 123, 124, 125, 130, 131, 163

O

office audit, 22, 26, 158, 165

OIC, 164, 165

ordinary and necessary, 40, 41, 42, 44, 47, 48, 50, 52, 54, 55, 58, 165

P

Penalty Abatement, v, 93, 116, 166

petition, 75, 84, 86, 89, 102, 111, 117, 121, 123, 124, 125, 126, 130, 131, 147, 164, 170

Prudence, 166, 167

Publication 1, 66, 128, 167

R

random, 17, 28, 167

reasonable cause, 116, 118, 168

reasonable collection potential, 97, 109

Revenue Agent, 10, 26, 27, 32, 76, 162, 168, 169

S

self-employed, 107, 170

statutory, 83, 85, 124, 130, 161, 163, 170

streamlined installment agreement, 170

substantiate, 43, 54, 107, 157

T

tax attorney, 94, 127

Tax Court, v, viii, ix, x, 75, 78, 82, 84, 85, 86, 89, 94, 102, 111, 117, 120, 121, 122, 123, 124, 125, 126, 127, 130, 131, 147, 153, 155

tax laws, 5, 83, 154, 162, 165

taxpayers, x, 4, 9, 19, 29, 33, 62, 63, 68, 89, 96, 106, 107, 108, 129, 153, 157, 159, 160, 162

U

United States Tax Court Practitioner, 94, 127, 173, 174

unlimited, 41, 78, 173

Made in the USA
Lexington, KY
18 May 2018